The Library of Author Biographies

Robert Cormier

The Library of Author Biographies

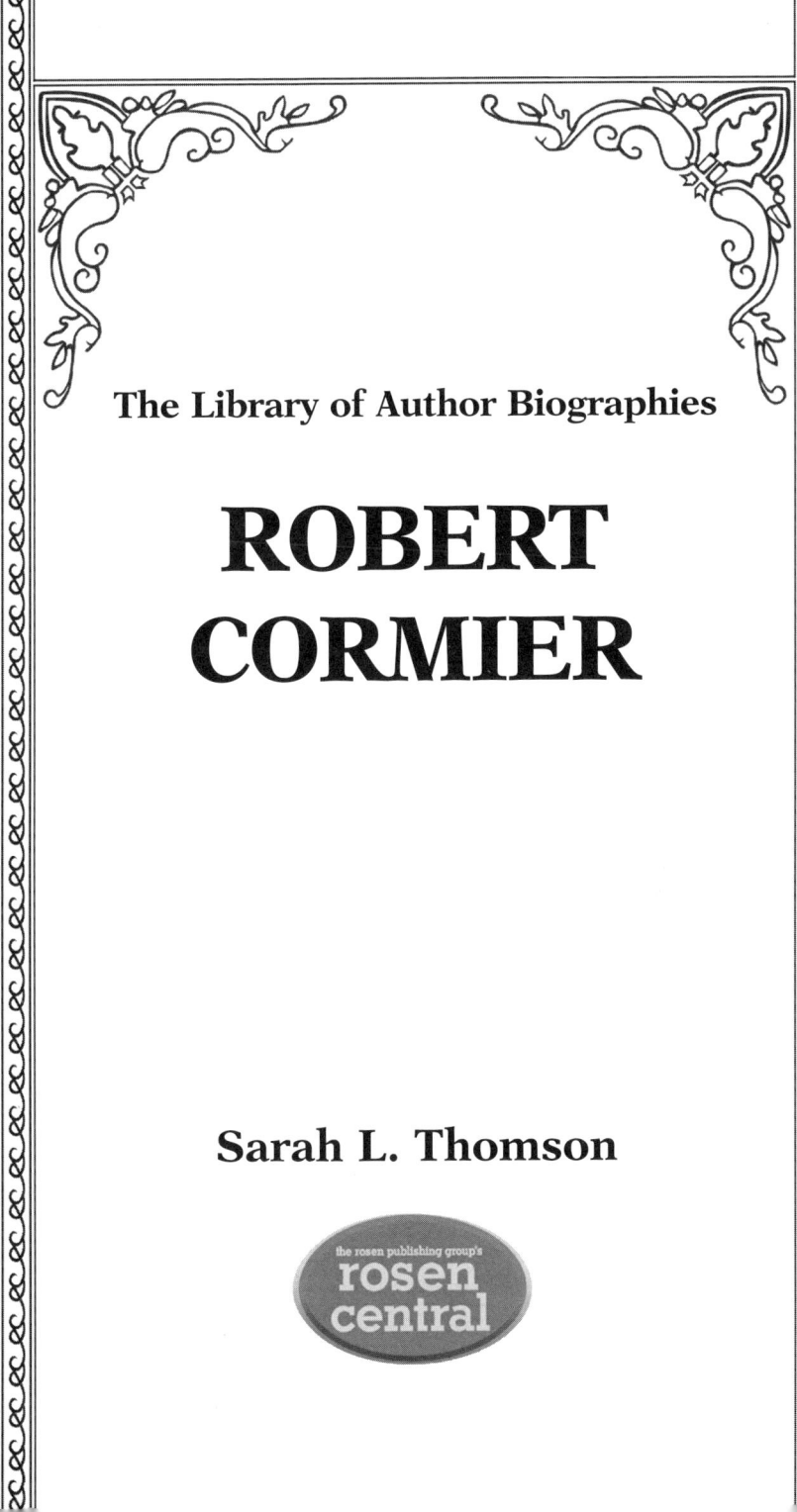

ROBERT CORMIER

Sarah L. Thomson

the rosen publishing group's
rosen central

Published in 2003 by The Rosen Publishing Group, Inc.
29 East 21st Street, New York, NY 10010

Copyright © 2003 by The Rosen Publishing Group, Inc.

First Edition

All rights reserved. No part of this book may be reproduced in any form without permission in writing from the publisher, except by a reviewer.

Library of Congress Cataloging-in-Publication Data

Thomson, Sarah L.
  Robert Cormier / by Sarah L. Thomson.— 1st ed.
    p. cm. — (The library of author biographies)
  Includes bibliographical references (p.) and index.
  ISBN 0-8239-3776-3
  1. Cormier, Robert. 2. Novelists, American—20th century—Biography. 3. Young adult fiction—Authorship. 4. Cormier, Robert. I. Title. II. Series.
  PS3553.O653 Z78 2002
  813'.54—dc21

2002007954

Manufactured in the United States of America

Excerpt from *Beyond the Chocolate War* Copyright © 1993 by Robert Cormier. Reprinted by permission of Laurel-Leaf Books. All rights reserved.

Excerpt from *The Bumblebee Flies Anyway* Copyright © 1993 by Robert Cormier. Reprinted by permission of Laurel-Leaf Books. All rights reserved.

Excerpt from *The Chocolate War* Copyright © 1974 by Robert Cormier. Reprinted by permission of Knopf. All rights reserved.

Excerpt from *Eight Plus One* Copyright © 1991 by Robert Cormier. Reprinted by permission of Laurel-Leaf Books. All rights reserved.

Excerpt from *Fade* Copyright © 1988 by Robert Cormier. Reprinted by permission of Delacorte Press. All rights reserved.

Excerpt from *I Am the Cheese* Copyright © 1977 by Robert Cormier. Reprinted by permission of Knopf. All rights reserved.

Table of Contents

Introduction: The War	7
1. Growing Up in "Monument," Massachusetts	15
2. "I Didn't Belong"	23
3. Writing a Life	30
4. A New Audience	39
5. Author at Work	50
6. The Creation of Evil	58
7. The Pull of the Dark	66
Interview with Robert Cormier	71
Timeline	77
Selected Reviews from *School Library Journal*	79
List of Selected Works	86
List of Selected Awards	88
Glossary	90
For More Information	93
For Further Reading	94
Bibliography	95
Source Notes	99
Index	110

Introduction: The War

"They murdered him."[1]

The opening line of Robert Cormier's *The Chocolate War* warns readers that they're not in for a pretty story. Though not a single character dies, Robert Cormier's first novel for teenagers is still about a murder—the murder of freshman Jerry Renault. By the end of the book, Jerry has been beaten and brutalized until he believes there's no point in trying to do the right thing. Even though he is not literally dead, Jerry has still been murdered, because he has given up hope.

Remarkably, *The Chocolate War* is about unimportant things—or things that should not be important. A war over chocolate? Why is a box of chocolates worth murdering Jerry Renault?

The answer is because the chocolates in question represent power at Jerry's Catholic high school, Trinity. Brother Leon, who is temporarily in charge at Trinity, thinks that if he can make a success of the chocolate sale, he'll be promoted to headmaster. Archie Costello, leader of a secret society called the Vigils, decides to use the chocolate sale to show Leon who truly runs the school. Archie is called the Assigner; he invents cruel practical jokes and orders the other students to participate. Jerry's assignment is simple: He must refuse to sell the chocolates for a week.

Jerry obeys. Leon is panicked; Archie is delighted. But when the week is up, Jerry still refuses to sell the chocolates, even though Archie now tells him to. He is tired of taking orders, tired of blindly obeying. Jerry has a poster in his locker with a single question on it, a quotation from the poet T. S. Eliot: "Do I dare disturb the universe?" Jerry decides to disturb the universe of Trinity School. He will not sell the chocolates.

Jerry isn't causing any harm. He isn't even breaking a rule. But he has said no to the two powers of Trinity School. Unless he is punished, his behavior may lead the other students to

Introduction: The War

question the authority of both the administration and the Vigils, and neither Leon nor Archie can afford to let that happen.

With the cooperation of Leon and the rest of the students, Archie tricks Jerry into a fight with the school bully, a fight Jerry cannot possibly win. No one comes to help Jerry as he is beaten to the ground.

As Jerry, who is badly injured, is held in the arms of his only friend at Trinity, he tries to speak. He wants to tell his friend "to sell the chocolates, to sell whatever they wanted you to sell, to do whatever they wanted you to do . . . Don't disturb the universe."[2]

Many people were upset by *The Chocolate War* when it was published. Reviewers objected to the violence in the book, to its use of swear words, to its frankness about sexuality, to the lack of adults that readers could admire. They were disturbed by scenes like Jerry's fight with the bully, Janza, which was watched by his friend, the Goober.

> Horrified, the Goober counted the punches Janza was throwing at his helpless opponent. Fifteen, sixteen. He leaped to his feet. Stop it, stop it. But nobody heard. His voice was lost in the thunder of screaming voices, voices calling for the kill . . . kill him, kill him. Goober

watched helplessly as Jerry finally sank to the stage, bloody, opened mouth, sucking for air, eyes unfocused, flesh swollen. His body was poised for a moment like some wounded animal and then he collapsed like a hunk of meat cut loose from a butcher's hook.

And the lights went out.[3]

But most of all, reviewers objected to the hopeless ending. *Booklist*, a magazine published by the American Library Association, enclosed a review of *The Chocolate War* in a black border, traditionally used for notices of death, and gave the review a title: "Whammo, you lose."

> Robert Cormier's *The Chocolate War* . . . is a book that looks with adult bitterness at the inherent [natural] evil of human nature and the way young people can be dehumanized into power-hungry and blood-thirsty adults.
>
> The author drives his point home over and over with a jackhammer style that leaves no pause for the characters to develop into real human beings of mixed emotion and action . . . Cormier is good at building and playing on dread. With a powerfully stacked plot and see-through characters, he manipulates readers into believing how rotten things are by loading the dice while pretending to play fair. See these regular old dice? Whammo, you lose."[4]

Introduction: The War

Another critic, Norma Bagnall, wrote an article about *The Chocolate War* in *Top of the News*, a magazine also published by the American Library Association. Bagnall objected to *The Chocolate War* because "it presents a distorted view of reality and a feeling of absolute hopelessness that is unhealthy."[5]

> There are no adults worth emulating [imitating]; Jerry is the only decent kid, and he is victimized by his peers, with the cooperation of school officials. Only the ugly is present through the novel's language, action, and imagery; goodness and honor are never rewarded . . . It is not appropriate for young people because it presents a distorted view of reality and because it lacks hope.[6]

But the book also had its defenders. Richard Peck, a highly regarded author of books for young adults, wrote a review calling *The Chocolate War* "the most uncompromising novel ever directed to the '12 and up reader'—and very likely the most necessary."[7] Two other writers collaborated on a reply to Bagnall in the next issue of *Top of the News*, arguing that she had misinterpreted Cormier's work. A librarian wrote a letter in response to Bagnall's article, which argued that, "If we give young adults only those books described by Norma Bagnall as being desirable, which would give students adults worth emulating [imitating], show goodness and honor being rewarded, detail situations where hope is proved right, I suggest that *that* would present a warped view of the world. Young adults must learn that if they are going to stand firm for something, there will be times of absolute aloneness . . . There will be times of having no hope of any kind. Learning that virtue is its own and only reward is important."[8]

Robert Cormier himself was surprised at the controversy. "Frankly, I was astonished at the reception of *The Chocolate War* when people started talking about its downbeat philosophy,"[9] he said in a later interview. To Cormier, the ending of *The Chocolate War* was simply the logical outcome of the situation and characters he had created. "When I began writing it, I just wanted to set the situation up and then the characters become real to me," he explained. "In every story, once an author has established the people and the situations, there's an air of inevitability about it that can't be tampered with."[10]

The Chocolate War continued to be controversial long after its publication. The American Library Association keeps track of "challenges,"

Introduction: The War

when individuals or organizations try to remove, or ban, a particular book from a library or a school. In the years between 1990–2001, *The Chocolate War* was fourth on their list of most frequently challenged books. Parents objected to their children reading it in class. Organizations like the conservative group Family Friendly Libraries tried to get the book removed from library shelves.

Cormier's later works became the targets of censorship as well. In Panama City, Florida, in 1985, two parents objected to the assignment of Cormier's second novel, *I Am the Cheese* (1977) in their daughter's class at Mowat Junior High School. Their protest touched off a three-year battle over which books could be taught in the school. The teacher who led the fight against the book banning received a death threat; a reporter covering the story was also threatened and had her apartment set on fire, luckily without serious damage. In the end, not just *I Am the Cheese* but works by Shakespeare, Charles Dickens, Ernest Hemingway, and John Steinbeck were removed from the classrooms at Mowat Junior High.

After *The Chocolate War*, Robert Cormier went on to write eighteen more books for teenagers and to defend his right—and every author's right—to present difficult situations and less-than-perfect endings in books written for young readers. "I don't think having a happy ending should be one of the requirements of a children's book," he said in an interview. "Kids want their books to reflect reality, and they knew that the good guys don't always win."[11] He reminds his critics that keeping tragedy out of young people's books will not keep tragedy out of their lives. As Cormier says:

> Many adults, and certainly most parents, have a natural tendency to protect children. But unfortunately, this impulse often leads parents to attempt to control the entirety of their children's lives. This is not only wrong-headed; it's impossible . . . These parents don't seem to realize that kids live part of their lives outside of home and the classroom. They are part of the world. They watch television, ride buses, see newspaper headlines, and go to movies. Most kids have heard of corruption or terrorism or sexuality, and I see no reason not to deal with these subjects in children's books.[12]

1 Growing Up in "Monument," Massachusetts

Few readers of Robert Cormier's books have ever been to Leominster, Massachusetts, where Cormier lived for most of his life. But they are familiar with it all the same, because the town of Monument—the setting for most of Cormier's books—is "a thinly disguised Leominster."[1]

Robert Cormier grew up in a neighborhood of Leominster called French Hill (familiar to his readers as Frenchtown), a community of French Canadian immigrants established in the early years of the 1900s. Cormier's grandfather was born in Canada, moved to French Hill, and found work in a factory where combs were made of celluloid, an early form of plastic. His son, Lucien Joseph Cormier, also went to work in the comb factory. He would work there for forty-two years.

In his novel *Fade* (1988), Robert Cormier described a factory like the one where his father and grandfather worked.

> You opened the door of the Rub Room at the comb shop and a blast like purgatory struck your face. The workers sat on stools, huddled like gnomes over the whirling wheels, holding the combs against the wheels to smooth away the rough spots. The room roared with the sound of machinery while the foul smell of the mud soiled the air. The mud was a mixture of ashes and water in which the wheels splashed so that they would not overheat at point of contact with the combs. Because the Rub Room was located in the cellar of the shop where there were no windows, the workers toiled in the naked glare of ceiling lights that intensified everything in the room: the noise, the smells, the heat, and the cursing of the men. On the coldest day of the year, the temperature of the Rub Room was oppressive; in the summer, unbearable.[2]

Joseph Cormier married Irma Collins, a young woman of Irish background. They had eight children; Robert Edmund, known as Bob to his family, was the second, born on January 17, 1925.

Bob had an older brother, Norman, and six younger siblings: Leo, Gloria, John, Anne, and twins Constance and Charles. Joseph and Irma Cormier lived for a while in the ground floor of a tenement, a three-story building, owned by Joseph's father. Bob's grandparents lived on the top floor. Aunts and uncles and cousins were nearby. Bob's family moved often when he was young, since they needed larger apartments as more and more children were born. But they always stayed in French Hill, and family was always close.

Cormier's family did not have much money. The only income was Bob's father's salary, and during the Great Depression, when Bob was growing up, that salary was a small one for a large family. But the lack of money didn't worry him. "The neighborhood was a poor one by some standards and the Depression was the pollution of our lives," Cormier wrote later.

> Wednesday was payday, and if your father had worked a full week someone would be sent to the drugstore after supper for those two-for-a-nickel ice-cream cones. We'd sit on the piazza steps—we always called it a piazza, never a porch—and life was suddenly unbearably sweet. The secret, of course, was this: We didn't know we were

poor, simply because we didn't know anyone who was rich.[3]

Cormier had fond memories of his close-knit family. His grandfather was "a cheerful man who liked horses and cowboy pictures and grandchildren," and took his grandchildren for rides in "what was probably the last horse and team in town."[4] His father brought home Christmas trees that he had bought for bargain prices. Usually, they were lopsided and ragged, or they shed needles all over the floor. One year, Bob's father even chopped branches off one side of the tree and glued them into holes on the opposite side. But he would insist that "all Christmas trees are beautiful,"[5] and, once the tree was decorated, the family would have to admit that it was true.

Cormier's family wasn't untouched by tragedy. When Bob was just five years old, his brother Leo, younger than Bob by two years, died. Cormier was too young to remember the brother he had lost, but he did remember being sent to find his grandfather and deliver the sad news, running through the streets of French Hill on "that desperate mission."[6]

Like most of the children of French Hill, Bob went to St. Cecilia's Parochial Grammar

School, where classes were taught in English in the morning and French in the afternoon. Since the people of French Hill were the descendants of immigrants from the French-speaking province of Quebec, most of them spoke both French and English.

The classes at St Cecilia's were taught by nuns, and Bob found some of the religious instruction frightening. "It was a very oppressive faith that I had," he remembered later. "It was a theology of fear rather than love. I was good because I was afraid not to be."[7] The weekly confession in St. Cecilia's Church was particularly nerve-wracking. The confessionals, small, curtained alcoves where the students would tell a priest their sins, were close to the pews where the rest of the class waited. One of the priests was hard of hearing, and Bob would have to recite his sins loudly. "I was always aware of that thin curtain separating me from others nearby in the pews, fearing that someone would hear my innermost secrets,"[8] he remembered.

Bob also sang in the church choir at St. Cecilia's, a fact connected to an incident he remained angry about for years; when he was still quite young, it was decided that he had to have his tonsils taken out. He was wheeled into the operating room and the nurse, who had learned somehow that Bob liked to sing, asked if he would give them a song. Flattered and pleased, Bob opened his mouth—and the anesthetic mask was forced down over his face. "They tricked me!" he remembered. "I thought they loved me because I sang, and they tricked me. I'll never forget it. Authority sucks you in, and then—!"[9]

But Bob's experiences at St. Cecilia's weren't all bad, and some of the teachers there encouraged his growing talent for writing. He had always loved to make up stories. "I can't remember a time, really, when I haven't been a writer,"[10] he said. But he began to take his writing more seriously when, in the seventh grade, he wrote a poem for one of his teachers, Sister Catherine. She read the poem carefully and said, "Why, Bob! You are a writer!"[11] Her praise helped Bob to think of himself as an author, someone who could someday make a living with words.

On Bob's twelfth birthday, an aunt gave him the first book, other than a textbook, he had ever owned: *The Adventures of Tom Sawyer* (1876). He read it over and over, fascinated by Mark Twain's story of boyhood in a small Missouri town. After reading *Tom Sawyer*, Bob asked the librarian if he could have an adult library card, rather than a card that restricted him to books in the children's section. He began to read authors who would have a great influence on him, like William Saroyan and Thomas Wolfe. "During Depression winters," Cormier remembered about the boy he had been, "he lay on the floor near the black Barstowe stove and flew the trapeze with Saroyan's daring young man and stalked the streets with Thomas Wolfe's young writer seeking fame and fortune."[12]

Bob also read comic books and short stories in magazines like the *Saturday Evening Post*. He loved movies, and every week he went to the Saturday matinee. "The boy I used to be would leave the theatre late on a Saturday afternoon in the waning daylight and walk down the street with the John Wayne kind of swagger," Cormier remembered. "Those were marvelous moments—moments of sweetness and innocence when the bad guys appeared only in your daydreams and the good guys always won."[13] His mother had given up going to the movies, and Bob would come home and tell her the plot of each film he'd seen. He didn't realize it at the time, but he was learning to be a storyteller, training his eye and ear for plot and dialogue. Later he would credit these movies with helping him to learn how to set up a story.

Bob found another way to satisfy his need for drama. On spring evenings, he sometimes dressed up with a pillowcase for a mask and a blue bedspread for a cape and ran through the backyards of French Hill. The kids in the neighborhood called this mysterious figure "the ghost." "The ghost would pause in his solitary majesty," Cormier remembered. "The hiding kids would venture [risk going] forth, tempting the fates, edging near—and then he would explode again in that marvelous laughter and chase them once more, and the springtime evening was suddenly touched with magic."[14] He would also wrap himself up in an old bedspread and tell ghost stories to the younger children in the neighborhood in the basement of his parents' house.

Like the younger children of French Hill, Bob's mother was an appreciative audience for his stories. "He would scribble something on a scratch pad on the kitchen table," Cormier wrote about himself, "and rush to read it to this beautiful woman who was not only his mother but someone who listened and shook her head with wonder and said: 'That's fine, that's just fine. You're going to be a real writer someday, mark my words.'"[15]

2 "I Didn't Belong"

Bob's life in French Hill seemed simple and comfortable. He had a close family and a good friend, Pete Dignard. Pete and Bob went to the movies together, played baseball, and collected empty soda bottles to sell for two cents each. Pete listened to Bob's dreams about a beautiful girl he'd glimpsed in downtown Leominster and followed to her house, not daring to speak to her. But as a boy who liked to read and who didn't love sports, Bob didn't fit in well with the other students at St. Cecilia's. Despite Pete's companionship and the love of his family, he often felt out of place and alone. "On the surface it looked like a very pleasant, ordinary [adolescence]," Cormier said.

I came from a warm and loving family, really, and I went to parochial school and on into high school. But between the lines there is the fact that I always felt that I didn't belong. I was easily intimidated [frightened]: on my paper route, being chased by dogs or going into certain neighborhoods intimidated me. I was a pretty timid kid.[1]

Maybe it was Bob's timidity that made him easy prey for a bully who tormented him when he was twelve or thirteen. Bob had seen the older boy around the neighborhood, but didn't know much about him. He certainly never knew why the bully decided to threaten him and chase him through the streets of French Hill. "We never spoke a word," he remembered, "but he looked at me with such a glitter of triumph and with such malice that instinctively I would head the other way."[2] Because Bob was a fast runner and he knew all the shortcuts and hiding places in French Hill, the bully never caught him. But this didn't make Bob any less fearful. Eventually, the older boy lost interest; Bob never knew why, just as he never knew exactly what had made the bully start to chase him in the first place.

A year or so later, when Bob was fourteen and in eighth grade, his family lived in a rented house so close to St. Cecilia's that Bob could see the house from his classroom window. One day, near the end of the school year, Bob looked out of the window and saw a house on fire—his own. He knew that his mother and his baby sister were at home. Horrified, he leapt out of his seat, but his teacher stopped him before he could run out the door and she insisted that he say several prayers before going home. The teacher must have believed the prayers were very important, but each second that ticked by was torture for Bob, who was desperate with anxiety for his family. Luckily, no one was hurt in the fire, but Cormier's anger over his teacher's insensitivity lingered for years.

Eighth grade was the last grade at St. Cecilia's, and graduation night was a festive occasion. The suit Bob was going to wear for graduation had been destroyed in the fire that burned down his family's home, but the neighbors in French Hill had all contributed to buy clothes for Bob and the rest of his family. Their generosity meant that Bob was able to wear a suit to his graduation after all.

Students from St. Cecilia's continued their schooling at the public junior high school. This was often a difficult transition because most of the other students had been at the junior high since seventh grade. The St. Cecilia students entered as ninth graders and would spend only one year there before going on to high school. In addition, nearly all the students at St. Cecilia's were French Canadian Catholics, a group that was sometimes called (or who called themselves) Canucks. At the junior high, which was attended by students from all over Leominster, the St. Cecilia students were suddenly in the minority. Bob also graduated from St. Cecilia's a year ahead of his good friend, Pete Dignard, and gradually lost touch with him.

Paul Roget, the protagonist of Cormier's novel *Fade* (1988), transfers from a small Catholic school to a public junior high just as Cormier did. (Cormier describes Paul as "the most autobiographical character I've ever created."[3]) At first, Paul is enthusiastic about the new place, but he soon discovers that his cousin Jules feels differently.

> "We don't belong there," he said. "We'll never catch up." By this he meant that we were joining the school in the ninth grade, and would be leaving at the end of the year for Monument High. "These kids have been together since the first grade. My homeroom teacher called Raymond LeBlanc a Canuck. But not in a nice way. Said it like it was a dirty word . . ."

"I Didn't Belong"

"They've got a school magazine," I said. "A literary magazine. Anyone can submit stories and they'll print them if they're good enough."

Jules stopped walking and turned to me.

"You're a Canuck, Paul. I don't think your stories will ever be good enough for them."[4]

Because the junior high and, later on, the high school, were so diverse, Bob was exposed to new experiences and opportunities. For example, it was in high school that Bob met a Jewish girl—the first time he had known someone of that religion—and the two of them had a series of long, intense conversations, sharing what they knew about their faiths. He also took part in high school plays and won a best acting award for his performance in *The Devil and Daniel Webster*. And he continued to write. Several of his teachers recognized his talent and encouraged him, and some of Bob's poetry was published in the local paper, the *Leominster Daily Enterprise*. However, Bob dreamed of something more. "The boy I remember didn't want to be either rich or poor, but he wanted to be known," Cormier wrote later. "The boy would ache with the loneliness of those who are unheralded and unsung. He wanted the world to know he existed, that he was there, that he was somebody!"[5]

27

Home continued to be a place of comfort for Bob when school was difficult. After many years of moving from one rented house to another, Bob's father was finally able to afford a house of his own. For a factory worker who was the son of an immigrant, the security and success this represented was enormous. During the summer when negotiations for the sale of the house were going on, Bob's father would often disappear from their home in the evenings. Later, his family learned that he would simply sit on a stone wall across the street and look at the home he was hoping to buy for himself and his family.

Cormier graduated from high school in 1942, in the middle of World War II. Many of his classmates went to serve in the military, but Cormier was too nearsighted. Instead, he got a job in a comb factory similar to the one in which his father had worked. The work was difficult, but "shop life was not all bad," Cormier remembered. "There's the camaraderie [companionship] of working together, shop picnics, and holidays. But I knew it was not for me."[6] He worked a night shift so that he could attend classes at Fitchburg Teachers College in a nearby town during the day.

One of his teachers at the college, Florence Conlon, was impressed by his writing and asked to see some of his fiction. Cormier showed her a short story, "The Little Things That Count." A few weeks later, Conlon came to see Cormier with a check for seventy-five dollars in her hand. Without telling him, she had had his story typed up and submitted to *The Sign*, a Catholic family magazine, which had accepted it. At the age of nineteen, Robert Cormier was a published author.

3 Writing a Life

Cormier didn't finish his courses at Fitchburg Teachers College. In 1946, at the age of twenty-one, he quit school to take a job writing radio commercials for station WTAG in Worchester, Massachusetts. It wasn't exactly the fame and fortune he had dreamed of, but it was a full-time writing job. While he was working at the radio station, he met Constance Senay at a dance.

Constance, called Connie, was from French Hill and though she had been two years behind Cormier in high school, the two did not know each other well. Because she was a friend of his sister Gloria, Cormier politely asked her to dance—and romance struck. The couple didn't separate for the next three dances. Soon afterward, they were going steady, seeing each other regularly. And in 1948, after Cormier got a new job, they were married at St. Cecilia's Church on November 6. It would be a stable, solid, loving marriage lasting for more than fifty years. "Love reveals itself in small ways," Cormier wrote. "I mean, you can make big heroic gestures and buy her flowers every once in a while, or remember birthdays and anniversaries and go wild with a shopping list at Christmas, but it's the little things that make up love."[1]

Cormier's new job was on the night staff of the *Worchester Telegram and Gazette*. He worked there as a reporter for seven years; during this time, his first two children were born, Roberta in 1951 and Peter in 1953. While his children were still young, Cormier found that his feelings about religion were changing. His Catholic faith had always been a powerful force in his life, but during this period, Cormier had met a priest who was "a man of joy," and this helped, Cormier said, to change "my belief to one of joy rather than one of fear."[2] Catholicism also underwent many changes in the early sixties, bringing a new openness and tolerance to the church. Because of these changes, Cormier became more comfortable with

Catholicism, and religion remained important to him for his entire life. Although Cormier's religious faith is not obvious in any of his young adult novels, it underlies his seriousness about good and evil. *The Bumblebee Flies Anyway* (1983) is dedicated "to old pals, my saints, Jude Thaddeus, Martin and Anthony and a new one, Max, with thanks."[3] These are the saints that Cormier prayed to: Jude Thaddeus, the patron saint of lost causes; Martin, a black priest in South Africa; Anthony, the finder of lost things; and Maximillian Kobe, who died in a Nazi concentration camp, sacrificing himself so that another family could survive.

After seven years at the *Worchester Telegram and Gazette*, Cormier accepted a job with the *Fitchburg Sentinel*. He would work at this newspaper for the next twenty-seven years, as a reporter, an editor, and a columnist. During this time, he and Connie would have two more children: Christine, born in 1957, and Renee, born ten years later.

Cormier won three awards for his journalism. In 1959, when he was thirty-four, his story about a child burned in a car accident won the Associated Press Award of New England for the best human interest story of the year. In 1973, at forty-eight years old, he won the same award for an article about a workshop staffed by people with mental disabilities. A year later, in 1974, his human interest column was judged the best in the entire Thomson newspaper chain, the international company that owned his newspaper as well as many others.

Cormier started writing his column, "And So On," in the late 1960s. He used a pseudonym, John Fitch IV, a name borrowed from the founder of the town of Fitchburg. The use of a pen name gave him "the freedom to be personal without embarrassing anyone," his wife Connie wrote. Since no one knew who he was, he had "the ability to be outrageous, to take chances, to be sentimental, if he wished."[4]

Cormier wrote columns about current events, memories of growing up in French Hill, and his family, particularly his youngest daughter, Renee. His columns are attentive to the small details of life, affectionate about memories of the past, and appreciative about the joys of raising children. Even when he wrote about serious issues, there was still an optimism that might surprise readers who know Cormier as the man who took them inside the mind of a serial killer in *Tenderness*

(1997) or a teenage terrorist in *After the First Death* (1979).

> Keep the faith, baby, they say. And we keep it, although there's botulism [food poisoning] in the soup and mercury in the fish and metal in the cereal . . . The children have tracks in their arms and anguish in their souls and nightmares in their sleep . . . And funny thing, we keep it. We keep the faith because the smile lighting the face of a child is more radiant than springtime and makes us forget the anger in the air and the violence in the streets. Dawn dispels darkness every morning in an unending miracle of rebirth . . . Of course we keep the faith. We keep it because of another four-letter word—love, baby, love . . . No one ever died of sentiment or of too much tenderness. And if we are tender toward each other, we may survive, after all.[5]

Even while working all day at the paper, Cormier continued to write fiction, working at night and on the weekends. At first he wrote short stories, selling some to the Catholic magazine *The Sign*, which had bought "The Little Things That Count," and others to magazines like *Redbook*, *Woman's Day*, *McCall's*, and the *Saturday Evening Post*. Readers who only know Cormier's young adult novels would be surprised by the tone and subjects of his short stories. Patricia Campbell, author of a biography and critical study of Cormier's work, describes them as "gentle and warm, a little sad, sometimes almost sentimental. He wrote about the small happinesses and disappointments of human relationships."[6]

Even though Cormier was selling his stories to magazines regularly, he confessed later, "I never liked writing short stories that much. They're very demanding and difficult." He felt constrained by the limits on space. "In a novel you can move around and create people and have a good time," he explained. "You can't do that in a short story. Every word counts. You have to keep the forward thrust. You can't play with it."[7]

While he continued to write and sell stories, Cormier also experimented with longer works. His first finished novel was called *Act of Contrition*, a work for adults based on his own family's history. He sent it to a publishing house, Houghton Mifflin, which didn't accept it. (In fact, *Act of Contrition* was never published.) But an editor at Houghton Mifflin was impressed enough by Cormier's talent to recommend that he get an agent, someone who would submit his work to publishers. She suggested that he try the Curtis Brown Agency. Ultimately, Cormier was taken on as a client by a new agent there named Marilyn Marlow.

When Cormier was in his early thirties, his writing was profoundly affected by a tragic event: His beloved father died. Cormier had always been close to his family and his love for his father was powerful. Remembering a Christmas in his childhood when he had made the bittersweet discovery that Santa Claus was actually his father in a costume, Cormier wrote, "Later, of course, I realized that the man who was my father was a real Santa, in a thousand ways: all the gifts he gave me, those gifts of the spirit."[8]

His father died, painfully, within six months of receiving a diagnosis of lung cancer and enduring an operation that did not save him. "The earth should stop turning for a while or lightning should spilt the sky when a good man dies," Cormier wrote in one of his newspaper columns. "But nothing happens."[9]

Not surprisingly, Cormier dealt with his grief at the typewriter, turning out page after page about his emotions and memories. Finally, his agent called to ask why she hadn't gotten any stories from him lately. When Cormier explained that he had been writing about his father's death, Marilyn Marlow asked to see what he had created, and then suggested that, with a little revision, what Cormier had written could become a novel.

What had started as a private effort to deal with Cormier's grief turned into his first published novel, *Now and at the Hour*, published in 1960 by Coward-McCann. *Now and at the Hour* isn't strictly autobiographical; not everything that happens in the book happened in Cormier's own life. However, as the main character comes to terms with his own death, the novel conveys something of the intense emotions Cormier experienced when his father died.

In the next five years, Cormier published two more novels for adults: *A Little Raw on Monday Mornings* in 1963 and *Take Me Where the Good Times Are* in 1965. He also finished two other novels that were never published. By that time, Cormier's three oldest children were in their teens, a time Cormier described in an introduction to a collection of stories, *Eight Plus One* (1980).

> The house sang those days with the vibrant sounds of youth—tender, hectic, tragic, and ecstatic. Hearts were broken on Sunday afternoon and repaired by the following

Thursday evening, but how desperate it all was in the interim. The telephone never stopped ringing, the shower seemed to be constantly running, the Beatles became a presence in our lives.[10]

And then, on a September afternoon in the late 1960s, Cormier's son, Peter, fourteen years old and a freshman in high school, came home with twenty-five boxes of chocolates to sell.

4 A New Audience

Peter didn't want to sell the chocolates. It was as simple as that. There was no secret society at Peter's high school, as there is in *The Chocolate War*. Unlike Brother Leon, the headmaster was not an evil man bent on controlling his students' lives. Peter was just busy with his schoolwork and wanted to play football, which would take a lot of his time. He talked about the issue with his family and his father pointed out that he wasn't required to sell the chocolates. It wasn't an assignment for which he would receive a grade. Peter had a choice.

With a note from his parents saying that they supported his decision, Peter went back to school the next day and returned the chocolates to the headmaster. He was the only student who didn't participate in the sale. And nothing happened. Peter's decision was accepted by the headmaster and the other students. Everything was fine.

But Cormier started to wonder. He had worried about what would happen to Peter in his first year at the school if he set himself apart from the other students, even in such a small way. What if the headmaster had not accepted Peter's decision? What if there had been pressure from the other students? What if the chocolate sale had not been just a small fund-raiser but a struggle for power within the school?

When he started writing *The Chocolate War*, Cormier didn't think of it as a novel for teenagers. "I didn't give much thought to who was going to read it," he said. "Back then, I certainly didn't think of myself as a children's writer."[1] But with three of his children now teenagers, Cormier had become interested in the transitional time of life between childhood and adulthood.

Cormier worked on his fiction at home, on an old manual typewriter. His study was at one end of the dining room, open to the rest of the house and to the comings and goings of his family. Because he had insomnia, he worked late at night and would be sitting at the typewriter when Roberta, Peter, Christine, and later Renee came home from dates or time spent with their friends. It was a wonderful time to talk, and this helped Cormier stay connected to what was going on in his children's lives. "There's an intimacy in the night," he wrote, "and you can say things to each other at that hour that would be impossible at three o'clock in the afternoon."[2]

Cormier became fascinated with his children's lives and with the intensity of their emotions. "I realized that they were all really leading a life that was more exciting than mine," he said. "For them the emotional pendulum was swinging back and forth all the time."[3] For a while Cormier had been writing short stories about teenagers. (He thought of these, like his other short stories, as something adults would read.) The next logical step was a novel about a teenager, and Peter's experience with the chocolate sale gave Cormier the idea he needed.

When Cormier told his agent what he was working on, she said that it sounded like a YA novel. "YA" stands for "young adult," and it is now a common term in the world of children's publishing, but at the time, Cormier had never heard it before. Although there had been books like Louisa May Alcott's *Little Women* (1868) and Mark Twain's *The Adventures of Tom Sawyer* (1876) that were enjoyed by teenage readers, the first young adult book is usually considered to have been Maureen Daly's *Seventeenth Summer*, a romance of first love published in 1942. Although there were exceptions, most of the young adult books published in the 1940s and 1950s were either romances or adventure stories.

In the late 1960s, young adult books began to tackle more difficult and realistic subjects—death, violence, racism, poverty. In S. E. Hinton's novel *The Outsiders* (1967), unlike *Seventeenth Summer*, the characters aren't concerned with romance. These teenagers "didn't have time to agonize over first love and dates for the prom," author and critic Michael Cart wrote. "They were too busy agonizing over whether they would survive the next battle in their ongoing war with a rival gang."[4] These more realistic books helped to start a new trend, the "problem novel," which became very popular in the 1960s and 1970s. Focused on a single issue—perhaps alcoholism, abortion, suicide, drugs, broken families, or

A New Audience

child abuse—problem novels often had simple plots and shallow characterization, as if the author's attention were on teaching his or her readers a lesson rather than on the writing itself.

With its powerful, sophisticated writing, bleak tone, and unhappy ending, *The Chocolate War* was startlingly different from anything that had been previously published for young adults. When Marilyn Marlow sent the novel out, she encountered interest from several publishers, but she also met with resistance. One editor complained that there were too many characters to keep track of and wanted Cormier to cut the cast of the book by half. Another publisher offered Cormier a $5,000 advance, but only if he would change the book's ending. Cormier was tempted to accept, but in the end, he turned the offer down, knowing that a happy ending would not be true to the book he had created.

Finally, *The Chocolate War* was accepted by editor Fabio Coen at Pantheon Books. It was published essentially as Cormier had written it, with only one major change. Coen suggested removing a chapter that Cormier himself had doubts about; in fact, he had already taken this chapter out of the manuscript once and then put it back in. Once *The Chocolate War* was published, the reaction was extraordinary. Cormier was either praised for the stark realism of the book or criticized for its negative and hopeless tone. He was told both that he had written an important, groundbreaking book and something entirely inappropriate for young readers.

Cormier didn't let himself be unsettled by the uproar. "Actually, the critical response doesn't worry me," he said in an interview. "I've had very few reviews that have upset me."[5] Instead, he turned his attention to his next project. He spent some time on a sequel to *The Chocolate War*, but in the end put it aside, afraid that he was writing a second book because *The Chocolate War* had received so much attention and not because he had something new to say. He felt "emotionally bankrupt,"[6] with no new ideas or even strong feelings, unsure what to try next. One day, merely as an exercise, he began to write about a boy on a bicycle on a Wednesday morning.

> I am riding the bicycle and I am on Route 31 in Monument, Massachusetts, on my way to Rutterburg, Vermont, and I'm pedaling furiously because this is an old-fashioned bike, no speeds, no fenders, only the warped tires and the brakes that don't always work and the handlebars with cracked rubber grips

A New Audience

to steer with. A plain bike—the kind my father rode as a kid years ago. It's cold as I pedal along, the wind like a snake slithering up my sleeves and into my jacket and my pants legs too. But I keep pedaling, I keep pedaling.[7]

Immediately, Cormier began to wonder about the boy he had created. Why wasn't he in school? Why was he going to Rutterburg? What was in the package he carried? To answer these questions, he kept writing. As he wrote, he gave the boy—Adam—many of his own characteristics, especially his fears. For example, Adam is claustrophobic and uneasy around dogs, just like Cormier.

Cormier wasn't sure what to do with his pages about a boy on his bike; they didn't seem like a novel on their own. Then he read an article about the witness protection program, in which witnesses against powerful criminals are given new identities to protect them from people who might want to take revenge on them. Suddenly, they have new names, new family histories, new homes. Cormier was intrigued by the idea of inventing a different life. He put the concept of the witness protection program together with the story of the boy on the bike, and *I Am the Cheese* (1977) began to take shape.

I Am the Cheese is a complex, suspenseful novel. There is the opening story of the boy on the bike, going to visit his father. Then there are the mysterious transcripts, which seem to be records of a dialogue between someone who may be a psychiatrist and a patient suffering from a loss of memory. But why does the doctor seem so interested in what the patient's father may have known about a long-ago crime? And there are also the patient's memories of his previous life. It isn't until the final chapter that all these pieces come together. If readers are alert enough to pick up the clues, they can discover that the boy on the bike is the patient in the transcripts, except that he is more of a prisoner than a patient. He's trapped in a hospital or clinic, controlled by drugs and manipulated by a doctor who is really a government agent. There is no escape except in a fantasy of a bike ride that, in reality, goes nowhere.

"I felt like a mad doctor in a laboratory," Cormier says of writing *I Am the Cheese*. "I didn't think it would ever work, yet I felt compelled to write it."[8] At last Cormier sent the manuscript off to his editor, Fabio Coen. Cormier wasn't confident about its reception, worried that the new book was too complicated and perhaps not

A New Audience

even successful as a story. He included a note of apology with the manuscript, afraid of letting Coen down after the success of *The Chocolate War*. But Coen was enthusiastic and had no doubts that the book should be published as a young adult novel.

Some reviewers agreed with Cormier that the novel might be too complex for teenagers. One reviewer for the *Times Education Supplement* worried that the book might "do real harm to a disturbed adolescent"[9] since it portrayed a psychiatrist as the enemy. But others approved of *I Am the Cheese*. The *Times Literary Supplement* said that "beside it, most books for the young seem as insubstantial as candyfloss."[10] And a reviewer for *Horn Book*, a magazine dedicated to children's literature, declared that the novel was "a magnificent accomplishment . . . cunningly wrought, shattering in its emotional implications."[11]

With the publication of his first two novels for young adults, Cormier had found a new audience and a new subject. "For me, the adolescent mind is much more interesting to write about,"[12] he said. His children continued to keep him aware of the experiences of young adults, and after *I Am the Cheese* was published, he found another way to connect to his new readers. In the book, during his bike ride, Adam tries three times to call his friend Amy Hertz. Amy's number is printed in the book, and some readers, out of curiosity, tried calling it to see if anyone would pick up the phone. Someone did—the author himself.

Some who had made the call told others. As word spread that Amy's phone number was actually Cormier's, more and more readers called him, amazed that the man on the other end of the phone was the author of the book they had just been reading. Cormier was happy to discuss their questions about his books. Some readers played along with the fiction that the phone number was actually Amy's and asked to speak to her. Cormier would participate, saying that he was Amy's father. If his youngest daughter, Renee, answered the phone and readers asked for Amy, Renee would simply say, "Speaking."[13] This blurring between fiction and reality startled some callers so much that they hung up. Others enjoyed the pretense.

Many writers might be reluctant to publish their phone numbers, fearing that they will be overwhelmed with calls or become the victim of pranks. But Cormier enjoyed chatting with his readers. The phone calls and the many letters he received helped him stay connected to the world of adolescence.

I Am the Cheese and Cormier's first book, *The Chocolate War*, were both made into movies—*I Am the Cheese* in 1983 and *The Chocolate War* in 1988. Cormier was closely involved in writing the screenplay for *I Am the Cheese* and even had a small role as Amy Hertz's father, but the complex book didn't translate well to the screen, and the movie was withdrawn from theaters after a terrible reception from movie critics. *The Chocolate War* was more successful; Patricia Campbell, author of *Presenting Robert Cormier*, called it a "sensitive and respectful treatment,"[14] even though director Keith Gordon, who also wrote the screenplay, changed the ending to let Jerry confront Archie in the boxing ring and come out victorious.

But books, not movies, were the focus of Cormier's career. After *The Chocolate War* was published, he wrote very few short stories and no more works for adults. He concentrated on young adult novels for the rest of his life.

5 Author at Work

In 1978, a year after *I Am the Cheese* was published, Cormier quit his newspaper job to devote himself full-time to writing fiction. After a while, he settled into a routine. He would spend the morning at the typewriter, working anywhere from two and a half to four hours. In the afternoons, he took a break, perhaps visiting some friends or taking a drive or watching a television show he'd taped on the VCR. In the evenings, he would read over what he had written in the morning. "If it reads well, it makes me feel like writing again the next morning; and it if doesn't it still makes me feel like correcting the material,"[1] he explained.

Cormier followed the same general process in writing each of his novels. When he first sat down at his desk, he did not have an entire plot worked out in his mind. Instead, he would come up with an idea that was connected to a powerful feeling, such as the loneliness and desperation of Jerry Renault (*The Chocolate War*) as he stands alone against an entire school, or the fear and urgency of Adam Farmer (*I Am the Cheese*), frantically pedaling his bike to who knows where. "To work for me, an idea must be attached to an emotion, something that upsets, dazzles, or angers me and sends me to the typewriter,"[2] he explained.

Once he had a character—like Jerry or Adam—in mind, Cormier simply wrote about him, setting up different scenes and situations to discover how his character would respond. "I'm always telling myself as I write that I'm not really writing a novel; I'm just going to fool around with a character or an idea," he said.

"I also don't like to think in terms of writing ten or twelve pages a day. Usually I'm writing a scene, and it's always with the idea, 'I wonder what is going to happen'. . . I'm very disorganized at first; but finally it comes into a structure where consciously I'm working on a novel per se [as such]."[3]

Much of what Cormier wrote in his early drafts never ended up in his finished books. "The hundreds of discarded pages for *Beyond the Chocolate War* fill a huge cardboard box,"[4] he said, referring to his fourth novel for young adults, published in 1985. While he worked to revise a draft into a final manuscript, Cormier always kept his readers in mind. "You have to be ruthless with yourself and avoid self-indulgence," he explained. "You have to remember the reader, always."[5] And once a manuscript had been sent to an editor, Cormier was always open to suggestions for improvement. "One of my strengths has been my willingness to be guided by editors, to rewrite and listen to editorial suggestions," he said. "Once I've had the joy of writing the book, then I want it to be the best book possible for the reader."[6]

Constant reading helped Cormier learn his craft. He was always alert to the effect words on the page had on him. "I'm always asking as I read, 'How did the writer do this? Why do I suddenly have tears in my eyes? Why am I crying?'"[7] He looked at his own work in the same careful, critical way, well aware of his weaknesses. "I don't think I began to be a professional writer until I learned my weaknesses and what I couldn't do," he said. Cormier discovered, for example, that describing scenes was difficult for him. "I'm terrible at describing landscapes—trees, buildings . . . I always think, 'Oh no, here comes another building I have to describe.'"[8] He discovered that metaphors and similes allowed him to describe scenes without going into detail that was difficult for him. When he realized that, despite his ignorance of architecture, he could describe a luxurious mansion as "a big white birthday cake of a house," he felt "the way Columbus must have felt when he sighted land."[9]

Writing was a joy for Cormier. "There are so many rewards," he said. "When you get the ideas, that's a thrill; when you're writing the book and it's coming out well, that's a thrill; when you finish it and other people read it, that's a thrill."[10] But it was hard work as well. And despite his success, Cormier always worried that his talent might fail him. "All the time I am writing, I am haunted because I don't know whether the novel is working or not,"[11] he said. "I hope there is a next book. That's the big fear: losing your faculties. I'm always afraid I'll wake up some morning and it will all be gone."[12]

The first book that Cormier wrote after quitting his newspaper job was partly inspired by his daughter Renee. Just twelve at the time, Renee adored her father. Cormier began to think about the absolute trust that a child has for a parent, and what terrible things might happen if a parent were to use that trust for his or her own ends. He also had a character in mind that he called "the California Girl," a beautiful, blonde, popular teenager who seems to have the perfect life. But could she have weaknesses that she's hiding? How would she react under stress? The presence of Fort Devens near Leominster and a story in the news about a terrorist bombing came together with these ideas to produce Cormier's third novel, *After the First Death* (1979).

"I've always wanted to write a love story," Cormier said. "*After the First Death* I thought would be my adolescent love story."[13] But when terrorists from an unnamed country take a bus full of young children hostage, a love story doesn't have much of a chance. As the tension grows to a nearly unbearable level, the lives of three teenage characters intersect: Kate, the driver of the bus, Cormier's "California Girl"; Miro, a young terrorist, whose assignment is to kill Kate; and Ben, the son of the general attempting to defeat the terrorists. By the end of the novel two of these three characters are dead and readers are left with troubling questions about the nature of patriotism, courage, and innocence.

"It's a marvelous story, written in crackling prose," a reviewer for *Newsweek* wrote. "It deals thoughtfully with not only the topical issues of terrorism but power and its abuses, loyalty and betrayal, courage and fear."[14] Following *After the First Death*, Cormier put together a collection of previously published short stories, *Eight Plus One*, in 1980, and published a new novel, *The Bumblebee Flies Anyway*, in 1983. Then, more than ten years after the publication of *The Chocolate War*, he returned to Trinity School. *Beyond the Chocolate War* came out in 1985.

At first, Cormier resisted the idea of a sequel to *The Chocolate War*, mostly because he thought that sequels are "usually disappointing."[15] But he kept receiving letters from readers who wanted to know what happened after the book ended. Many asked about a minor character, Tubs Casper. Cormier began to write about Tubs and his girlfriend, Rita, and although most of these scenes didn't appear in the final book, they helped him enter into the story once again.

Cormier didn't want to bring Jerry Rennault back to Trinity. "It would be like rewriting *The*

Chocolate War,"[16] he said. But another character caught Cormier's imagination—Obie, the secretary of the Vigils and Archie's sometimes reluctant, sometimes enthusiastic assistant. "I always thought Obie was the most neglected character in the [first] book, probably the most poignant, and the one that I sympathized with," Cormier explained. "Obie was a tragic kid who went through his entire high-school career and had nothing to show for it, and he was aware of that."[17] Even in *The Chocolate War*, Obie has moments of rebellion against Archie's leadership. But he never takes any action against Archie— until the second book. A starred review in *Horn Book Magazine* said that *Beyond the Chocolate War* "is one of Cormier's finest books to date: combining the sense of immediacy that a good newsman can convey with the psychological insight of a mature writer."[18]

After *Beyond the Chocolate War*, Cormier published nine more books, most to appreciative reviews. They were not all what readers had come to think of as "typical Cormier": dark, realistic, and focused on the existence of evil. *Frenchtown Summer* (1999), for example, is a gentle, semi-autobiographical novel in unrhymed verse, looking back at Cormier's childhood in French

Hill and his relationship with his father. But the majority of Cormier's novels tackled the kind of subjects that readers had come to expect from his work: vicious vandalism and family disintegration in *We All Fall Down* (1993); a serial killer in *Tenderness* (1997); the nature of guilt in *The Rag and Bone Shop* (2001).

The Rag and Bone Shop was Robert Cormier's last book. The man who had been called "the grand master of the YA novel"[19] died on November 2, 2000, of complications from a blood clot. He was seventy-five years old and had written eighteen books for young adults and three for adults. An obituary notice in the magazine *School Library Journal* celebrated his quiet life and his remarkable achievements.

> The author of *The Chocolate War* was a gentle man who asked tough questions. He was a devout Catholic whose most famous novel depicts a parochial school where hatred and cruelty flourish. He was a gentle, self-effacing man who could create searingly evil fictional characters.[20]

And Cormier was something else as well: a writer whose commitment to realism—even when it is painful—made sure his books would be remembered after his death.

6 The Creation of Evil

In a study of Robert Cormier's works published in *The Lion and the Unicorn*, Nancy Veglahn wrote, "Robert Cormier is one of the few writers of realistic fiction for young adults who creates genuinely evil characters."[1] Cormier's villains have been a major factor in making him the controversial writer that he is.

"I think people are fascinated by Archie just as we've always been fascinated by evil,"[2] Cormier said, referring to Archie Costello, the cruel mastermind of the Vigils in *The Chocolate War*. As readers, we are appalled by what Cormier's villains do, and at the same time, we keep reading to discover what they will do next. His evil characters are even more frightening because they are often supposed to be the good guys—priests, teachers, government officials, doctors, military officers, parents, and friends. And in the end, they often get their way. This is what upsets many people about Cormier's work: The bad guys win.

How could Robert Cormier—a loving husband and father, and a small-town journalist—create some of the most terrifying villains in young adult literature? Not even the people who knew him best always understood the connection between the author and the evil characters he created. Once, after Cormier's wife, Connie, had been typing a manuscript for her husband, she came into his study and looked at him in bewilderment. "Who are you?" she asked. "We've been together all these years, but sometimes I wonder."[3]

Part of the reason Cormier's villains are so convincing is that they are very human, closely based on the author's own feelings and experiences. Cormier was frank about admitting that his evil characters were as much a part of him as his heroes were. "My characters do things that I would never do," he said, "and yet I must admit that in writing certain parts of *The*

Chocolate War and *Beyond the Chocolate War* I sat there with a gleeful look on my face. If I'm the good guy in my books I'm also the bad guy."[4] When asked which of his characters is his favorite, Cormier would sometimes answer, "Archie." "He is a terrific character," he admitted. "I really love him dearly."[5]

Cormier's villains represent things of which the author himself was afraid. "I am frightened by today's world, terrified by it," he admitted. "I think that comes out in the books. I'm afraid of big things . . . Big government frightens me; so does big defense. I think that those fears come out in *I Am the Cheese*."[6] But little things frightened and angered Cormier as well. He never forgot the nurse who had tricked him when, as a child, he had to have his tonsils taken out. He wrote often about bullies like the one who had tormented him as a young boy:

> [I] wonder what happens to bullies, anyway, when they grow up.
>
> Maybe they grow up to be bullies in other ways. Maybe they grow up to be the guy who cuts in front of others in his car. Or who backs into your car in the parking lot and drives away without stopping. Or who barges in front of everybody else who's waiting in line at the bank or the office.

Or maybe bullies grow up to be like everybody else—or become nice guys after all. Maybe they do.

But I don't think so.[7]

But strangely, the man who wrote books in which the bad guys usually win and justice is rarely, if ever, served, always insisted that his own view of life was positive. "I am, by nature, an incurable optimist," he wrote.

> When someone sees the bottle as half empty, I view it as half full.
>
> I never believe the bad-weather forecasts.
>
> And I always expect the parade to start on time.
>
> My favorite cartoon is the one that shows two prisoners manacled [chained] high on a wall with no obvious means of escape and one of the prisoners says: Now here's my plan . . .[8]

Could the man who created Brother Leon and Archie Costello really have been an optimist? A careful look at the way evil functions in Cormier's books shows that the situation isn't as simple as it might seem. The villains are usually successful and go unpunished, but the triumph of evil in Cormier's fictional world is never complete.

Although Cormier's good characters face terrible odds, they never stop struggling to resist what is evil, even if their struggles do not save them. Adam in *I Am the Cheese* clings to memories of his loving family. In *After the First Death*, Kate fights to the end against the terrorists who hold her hostage, even though she has almost no chance of escape. At the end of *The Chocolate War*, Jerry seems utterly defeated, but in the sequel, he reappears healed and even strengthened by his experiences at Trinity. Finally, at the very end of the book, Jerry decides that he will go back to the school to face Brother Leon and the Vigils. Cormier never wrote a third book describing Jerry's return to Trinity, but he did speculate about what his fate might have been. "I wanted Jerry to be the opposite of evil, to begin to have an aspiration to something greater than what's going on at Trinity," he said. "He'll probably go back to Trinity and go through a purgatory but be triumphant in the end even though he looks as if he's defeated."[9]

Cormier's villains themselves tell us that evil is not all-powerful. In *Beyond the Chocolate War*, Archie's assistant, Obie, makes a discovery: Evil happens only when people accept it. Villains succeed because nobody has the courage to hold them accountable for their actions. But evil doesn't have to be tolerated. Archie himself makes this point when Obie confronts him.

The Creation of Evil

"You blame me for everything, right, Obie? You and Carter and all the others. Archie Costello, the bad guy. The villain. Archie, the bastard. Trinity would be such a beautiful place without Archie Costello. Right Obie? But it's not me, Obie, it's not me . . . It's you, Obie. You and Carter and Bunting and Leon and everybody. But especially you, Obie. Nobody forced you to do anything, buddy. Nobody made you join the Vigils . . . Know what, Obie? You could have said no anytime, anytime at all. But you didn't . . . Oh, I'm an easy scapegoat, Obie. For you and everybody else at Trinity. Always have been. But you had free choice, buddy. Just like Brother Andrew always says in Religion. Free choice, Obie, and you did the choosing . . . "[10]

Obie could have quit the Vigils. The students at Trinity could have refused to carry out Archie's cruel assignments. The teachers could have stepped in to protect Jerry. But everyone at Trinity chooses instead to obey Archie, either because they are afraid of him or because they secretly enjoy the suffering he inflicts on others. Their choices give Archie his power. Cormier spelled this out very clearly in an interview: "The power of the leader comes from those who allow themselves to be led . . . Terrible things happen because we allow them to happen."[11]

If evil triumphed simply because it is more powerful than good, then Cormier's books would be hopeless. But this isn't the case. Evil only triumphs if people make the wrong choices, and this is where Cormier's optimism can be seen. If villains like Archie have their power because many people choose to obey them, then that power can be taken away if many people choose to resist.

It's certainly true that, in Cormier's books, people often make the wrong choices. Those who don't do evil themselves accept it or ignore it or even collaborate with it. People like Jerry who try to resist are often destroyed because nobody comes to their aid. Evil is very real and very powerful in Cormier's world. As in his favorite cartoon, the prisoners are chained to the wall. It's hard to see any chance of escape.

But escape is possible all the same, because Cormier's world, although dark, is not entirely hopeless. Evil is powerful, but it can be defeated if people accept their responsibility to come together and resist. In a response to Norma Bagnall's attack on *The Chocolate War*, librarian Betty Carter and associate professor of library science Karen Harris make this point:

"Robert Cormier does not leave his readers without hope, but he does deliver a warning: They may not plead innocence, ignorance, or prior commitments when the threat of tyranny confronts them. He does not imply that resistance is easy, but he insists it is mandatory."[12]

7 The Pull of the Dark

In 1991, at the age of sixty-six, Robert Cormier was awarded the Margaret A. Edwards Award; he was only the third writer to receive it. (The award had been given in 1988 to S. E. Hinton and in 1990 to Richard Peck.) The Edwards Award honors a writer's lifelong contribution to literature for young adults. Specifically, the award committee made note of *The Chocolate War*, *I Am the Cheese*, and *After the First Death*, saying that "Cormier's brilliantly crafted and troubling novels have achieved the status of classics in young adult literature."[1]

What makes Cormier's dark and disturbing books classics? What brings readers to his tales of corruption and violence, in which innocence provides no protection and evil brings no punishment? Part of the answer lies in Cormier's skill as a writer. Even his harshest critics were forced to admit that he knew how to use words. "Cormier knows his craft; he has written a compelling novel,"[2] Norma Bagnall wrote in her article denouncing *The Chocolate War*.

Cormier's newspaper work and his short-story writing were good training for writing novels. To ensure that a newspaper has enough space for every article, a reporter must keep to a precise number of words. Short-story writers also have to keep their manuscripts brief. Cormier learned to make every word count. "I write very quickly," he said, "and my big fear is boring people. I want them to read quickly, stopped in their tracks."[3]

And he was successful. From the first lines of Cormier's novels, readers are stopped in their tracks. "They murdered him"[4] (*The Chocolate War*). "Ray Bannister started to build the guillotine the day Jerry Rennault returned to Monument"[5] (*Beyond the Chocolate War*). "My name is Francis Joseph Cassavant and I have just returned to Frenchtown in Monument and the war is over and I have no face"[6] (*Heroes*—1998). It's hard to think of another writer whose opening lines have the attention-getting power of Cormier's.

Once they've grabbed the reader, Cormier's novels don't let go. He took care never to let his readers lose interest, and as a result, his books are tightly written, without a wasted word or an unnecessary scene, filled with a sense of tension that pulls a reader forward. "I want to keep the reader turning those pages," he said. "And I try to write the way I would like to read a book, so I create incident and conflict." Cormier was skilled at building suspense through a series of small climaxes, little revelations, or peaks of excitement within each chapter. "Rather than waiting for one big climax, I try to create a lot of little conflicts between people," he explained. "I try to create a series of explosions as I go along."[7]

Cormier used suspense to engage a reader's curiosity; we keep turning the pages of a Cormier novel because we want to know what will happen next. But Cormier also wanted readers to be emotionally involved, to feel sympathy for his characters and care about their fates. He called himself "an emotional writer"[8] and began each book with a character and a powerful emotion. "I wanted to bring to life people like Jerry Renault and Adam Farmer and poor Tubs Casper, who appears for only one poignant moment [in *The Chocolate War*]," he wrote. "[In *After the First Death*] I wanted to make the reader feel the mounting heat and pressure in that hijacked bus while a child trembled in the night. These were my first concerns."[9] Even as he explored serious themes about human nature, Cormier never forgot that a novelist is primarily a storyteller whose business is to create characters and events that his or her readers will care about. "The story comes first," he said. "The rest really is a bonus, that people can find things in my books to argue about. Or to teach or debate. Or even to be upset about. That's all an extra richness for me. I just want to tell a darn good story."[10]

But of course, there is an extra richness to Cormier's books, something to argue about and teach and debate, and certainly to be upset about. Cormier raises questions of good and evil that are complex and difficult, and he provides no easy answers. Should Jerry have sold the chocolates in *The Chocolate War*? What exactly happened to Adam at the end of *I Am the Cheese*? Is there a difference between Artkin the terrorist and General Briggs in *After the First Death*? Is

Paul in *Fade* a murderer? Cormier raises difficult problems and never offers simple answers. His books raise endless subjects for debate, and this is part of what makes them so fascinating.

Ultimately, what made Cormier's work so controversial is part of what makes it so powerful. Cormier doesn't give his characters (or his readers) happy endings. Some critics and readers find this terribly upsetting. Others find it simply true to life. Terrible things happen every day. Those in power abuse their power at times. Ordinary people often turn aside when they see sins committed. People who do wrong are not always punished. If one person stands up against tyranny, he or she may well be defeated. Cormier acknowledged these truths in his fiction, and what helped to make his work a subject of debate and a target for censorship also helped to win him a loyal readership and turn his books into classics.

"Robert Cormier is the single most important author in the history of young adult literature," said Michael Cart, an author and a critic. "He was the first who had the courage and the art to give us literature that offered readers the plain, unvarnished truth that there weren't always happy endings."[11]

Interview with Robert Cormier

This interview with Robert Cormier was conducted by Tom Bodett for the nationally syndicated public radio series, *The Loose Leaf Book Company*, produced by Ben Manilla Productions, Inc., of San Francisco. For more of this interview, visit www.looseleaf.org.

TOM BODETT: You may recall the nursery rhyme, "The Farmer in the Dell." It's full of heigh-hoes and derry-oes as the farmer takes a wife, the wife takes a child, the child takes a nurse, who takes a dog, who takes a cat. The cat takes a rat, the rat takes the cheese, and in the end, the cheese stands alone. In Robert Cormier's 1977 novel for young adults, *I Am the Cheese*, teenager Adam Farmer discovers that he and his family have been in the super secret Witness Protection Program since he was a toddler. Everything he believes about himself and his origins is a fiction, most of it dictated to his parents by the mysterious government man, Mr. Grey. In the course of a surreal and adventurous bike ride, from Monument, Massachusetts to Rutterburg, Vermont, Adam Farmer drifts in and out of reality in his quest for identity. We were fortunate to have author Robert Cormier in the studio with us recently, and I began our visit by reading a passage from *I Am the Cheese*.

> "He had awakened from sleep as if shot out of a cannon, out of the everywhere into the here and now. The room, the bed, the cold moonlight chilling the room. He was in the bed and aware of the cold sheets, but he was also suspended, isolated, inhabitant of an unknown land, an unknown world, and he, himself, unidentified, caught and suspended in time. Who am I? I am Adam Farmer. But who am I? I am Adam Farmer. But Adam Farmer was only a name, words, a lesson he had learned here in the cold room and in that other room with the questions and answers. Who is Adam Farmer? He didn't know. His name might as well have been

Interview with Robert Cormier

kitchen chair or cellar steps. Adam Farmer was nothing. The void yawned ahead of him and behind him with no constant to guide himself by. Who am I? Adam Farmer. Two words, that's all."

Well, Robert Cormier, welcome to the show.

ROBERT CORMIER: Thank you, glad to be here.

TOM BODETT: That passage I just read, Robert, is probably the quintessential teenage cry for identity, if I've ever read it anywhere.

ROBERT CORMIER: I know it. I think identity is so important to teenage people. And in this particular case, his entire identity has been obliterated completely. You know most people even know their names and where they live and where they go to school, but inside they're looking for that identity. But poor Adam Farmer is completely isolated. And I think that isolation that adolescents feel is paramount in their lives.

TOM BODETT: My guest is Robert Cormier, the author of *I Am the Cheese*, and many other fine books for young adults. Robert, it's been said about your books that they focus on the dark side of life. Why is that? Why do you go for the more brooding aspects of teenage life?

ROBERT CORMIER: I don't start out to do it. You know sometimes I think I'm going to write a nice, light comedy. But I think what drives me to the typewriter, and I still use an old typewriter, is the things that upset me about the world, and the violence and the intimidation, which of course, makes for a better drama. I mean, you don't often see good news on the front page. And a lot of teenagers, at least from the letters I get, and the phone calls, they think about the dark sides of themselves. I mean adolescence isn't a completely happy time. It's probably one of the most devastating times for a lot of kids. And they're not in control of their lives, they're not sure who they are, again we go back to identity, and they find themselves in this very strange and violent world. And so a lot of times, the darkness in my novels confirms the way they feel. They know that life isn't a series of happy endings, and so they're not really shocked when they read an unhappy ending in any of my books, because they figure that's the way life is. And I think that's probably why the book is still being read. It's hard to generalize about these things, but I just have that feeling from the letters and phone calls. You know my phone number happens to be in *I Am the Cheese*, and I get calls all the time. It's been going on ever since the book was published. I received a phone call one day from a young girl in a psychiatric institution, and she said Adam was the only person she could identify with. She really clutched the book and then tried the phone number, and we had a long talk about how this Adam in the book was really a reflection of her own life, even though the circumstances were much different.

TOM BODETT: You know after all this time, twenty-three years, and I don't know how many books you've written since you wrote *I Am the Cheese*, what's the most interesting thing to you still about this, when you pick it up and hold it in your hands?

ROBERT CORMIER: I just picked it up over the weekend, knowing that we were going to be speaking, and at this point, it's almost as if someone else wrote it, because the reader only sees what's on the page. The reader doesn't see how far you've failed to reach what you tried to do. And some of my writings, I reread them and think I could have reached a higher potential in it, but *I Am the Cheese* is one of those happy things that I don't think, and this probably sounds very egotistical, but I don't think I could improve on it.

It was one of those books that set out do to what I wanted to do, and when I read it now, I kind of marvel, as if someone, a much better writer than I am, wrote that book twenty-three years ago.

TOM BODETT: Oh that's got to feel good.

ROBERT CORMIER: Yeah. It's a great feeling. 'Cause you don't feel like that about everything you write.

TOM BODETT: No, probably not.

ROBERT CORMIER: 'Cause you're always striving for that better word, that better phrase, that better metaphor.

TOM BODETT: Well the book is *I Am the Cheese*. Robert Cormier, it's been a real pleasure talking to you.

ROBERT CORMIER: Thank you, it's been my pleasure, really.

TOM CORMIER: *I Am the Cheese* is for young adults. It, along with Cormier's book, *The Chocolate War*, are often challenged by parents and concerned citizens in schools and libraries, which usually tells you two things. The books are pretty close to truth, and they're pretty darn good.

Timeline

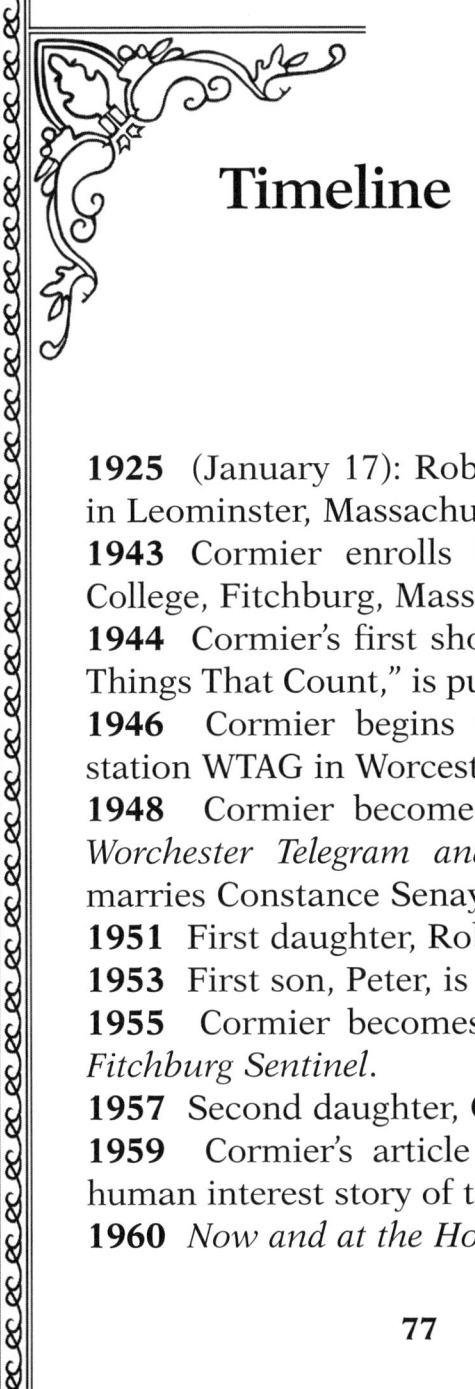

1925 (January 17): Robert Cormier is born in Leominster, Massachusetts.
1943 Cormier enrolls in Fitchburg State College, Fitchburg, Massachusetts.
1944 Cormier's first short story, "The Little Things That Count," is published in *The Sign*.
1946 Cormier begins work for the radio station WTAG in Worcester, Massachusetts.
1948 Cormier becomes a reporter at the *Worchester Telegram and Gazette*. Cormier marries Constance Senay.
1951 First daughter, Roberta, is born.
1953 First son, Peter, is born.
1955 Cormier becomes a reporter for the *Fitchburg Sentinel*.
1957 Second daughter, Christine, is born.
1959 Cormier's article is named the best human interest story of the year.
1960 *Now and at the Hour* is published.

1963 *A Little Raw on Monday Morning* is published.
1965 *Take Me Where the Good Times Are* is published.
1967 Third daughter, Renee, is born.
1973 Cormier's article is named the best human interest story of the year.
1974 *The Chocolate War* is published. Cormier's column named the best in the Thomson Newspapers chain.
1977 *I Am the Cheese* is published.
1979 *After the First Death* is published.
1980 *Eight Plus One* is published.
1983 *The Bumblebee Flies Anyway* is published.
1985 *Beyond the Chocolate War* is published.
1988 *Fade* is published.
1990 *Other Bells for Us to Ring* is published.
1992 *Tunes for Bears to Dance To* is published.
1993 *We All Fall Down* is published.
1995 *In the Middle of the Night* is published.
1997 *Tenderness* is published.
1998 *Heroes* is published.
1999 *Frenchtown Summer* is published.
2000 On November 3, Cormier dies of complications from a blood clot.
2001 *The Rag and Bone Shop* is published.

Selected Reviews from *School Library Journal*

I Am the Cheese
May 1977

Gr 8 Up—[*I Am the Cheese*] is a horrifying tale of government corruption, espionage, and counterespionage told by an innocent young victim. Adam Farmer's mind has blanked out; his past is revealed in bits and pieces—partly by Adam himself, partly through a transcription of Adam's interviews with a government psychiatrist. Adam's father, a newspaper reporter, gave evidence at the trial of a criminal organization that had infiltrated the government itself. He and his family, marked for death, came under the protection of the supersecret Department of

Reidentification, which changed the family's name and kept them under constant surveillance. Now an adolescent, Adam is finally let in on his parents' terrible secret, just in time for him to participate in a final escape effort that brings disaster to his parents and that leaves Adam broken in mind and spirit and at the mercy of an utterly ruthless government agency. The story demands close attention in order to put together the parts of the puzzle, and its grimness is unrivaled by any hint of humor; but, the buildup of suspense is terrific.

Frenchtown Summer
September 1999

Gr 6 Up—A touching, almost nostalgic coming-of-age story. Set shortly after World War I in the Frenchtown section of industrial Monument, Massachusetts, the novel centers on Eugene whose twelfth summer is filled with new experiences. He falls in love for the first time (with a piano-teaching nun named Sister Angelica), gets a job, and sees his first airplane. Eugene also experiences a profound loss when his favorite uncle suddenly dies. His initial steps into adolescence prompt him to turn inward and think about the relationships in his life. He wishes he were closer to his father, whom he describes as being as "unknowable as a

foreign language." Like Karen Hesse's *Out of the Dust* (Scholastic, 1977) and Mel Glenn's stories in poetry, this novel is written completely in verse, and is as masterful as Cormier's prose. The vivid descriptions of the Frenchtown tenement are positively haunting. Readers will see the faces of the characters and feel Eugene's struggle to understand his emotions. Despite its early twentieth-century setting, *Frenchtown Summer* is not a historical novel. It is a sensitive, superbly crafted story of a boy's journey into self-awareness.
—Edward Sullivan, New York Public Library

The Rag and Bone Shop
September 2001

Gr 7 Up—Cormier revisits familiar psychological and temporal territories in this memorable novella that was finished, but unpolished, at the time of his death. It's the beginning of summer vacation after seventh grade for Jason when his neighbor and friend, seven-year-old Alicia Bartlett, is murdered. Even though there is no physical evidence linking him to the crime, Jason is a suspect because he is thought to be the last person to have seen her alive. An ambitious, outside police interrogator who has a reputation for being able to extract a confession in difficult cases is brought in. Although Trent comes to believe that Jason is innocent, he succumbs to pressures of a high-profile investigation and successfully coerces a confession. Unfortunately for Trent, Alicia's older brother Brad confesses, is arrested, and charged. The interrogator is left with a tattered reputation and in the shocking denouement, Jason realizes that he has become a person capable of contemplating and thus, he asserts, carrying out a murder. The suggestion seems to be that childlike innocence, when betrayed by powerful, manipulative adults, can be easily subverted. Readers are shown a psychotic killer in the process of becoming. However, Jason, Trent, and the book as a whole present more questions than answers. Readers will be compelled to keep turning the pages, but will never know why Brad killed Alicia or if Jason is really capable of such a crime. These are things only individuals can know as they explore the dark interior of their own rag-and-bone shops. —Joel Shoemaker, Southeast Junior High School, Iowa City, Iowa

Tenderness
March 1997

Gr 6 Up—Cormier is in top form in this chilling portrait of a serial murderer. Eric Poole has progressed from killing kittens, cats, and a canary to parents and unsuspecting young women. Now eighteen, he has paid for his mother and stepfather's murders with three years of juvenile detention and is ready to continue his "plan." Unfortunately, his looks and shallow charm are as pleasing on the outside as his character is ugly on the inside. The story unfolds through the eyes of two characters: Eric, and the luckless fifteen-year-old Lori, a runaway who met Eric once when she was twelve and is drawn to him like a moth to the flame. Even when she realizes his guilt, after he attempts to kill her, she cannot desert him. The ugliness of the story contrasts with the beauty of the language. Perfectly titled with characteristic irony, a sense of "tenderness" pervades this gripping tale. Where other, lesser writers would have screamed the story in full-blown tabloid prose, Cormier is the model of decorum. No overt blood and gore are needed for this author to terrify his readers. Eric is not an antihero. Sympathy is not so much for the undeserving villain, but for the society that spawned and neutered him. A meaty horror study that's a fine substitute for the anemic, but popular "Fear Street" books. —Marilyn Payne Phillips, University City Public Library, Missouri

Fade
October 1988

Gr 10–12—Those who find Cormier's novels bleak, dark, disturbing, and violent will not be disappointed with his latest. And true to his past, he has given readers a story with more twists and turns than a mile of concertina wire. The first half is set in Frenchtown, a working-class section of a Massachusetts town. The time is the 1930s, and the evocation of life among the French-Canadians (with marvelous names like Omer LaBatt and Rudolphe Toubert), who toiled in sweatshops where celluloid combs were made, is the best thing about the novel. Not that the storyline doesn't work. Cormier uses an old device that guarantees attention—a lead character who can make himself invisible. The rules for fading are as complicated as a missile defense treaty. Paul Moreaux is the teenage *fader* who narrates the first section, an autobiographical account written after he has become a famous novelist. Readers learn early on that there is a grim side to this gift of fading and that Cormier intends it to represent a potentially evil force within us all. Subsequent sections include a narration by a present-day female cousin, which throws into question the truth of the entire first section, and a concluding section that

Selected Reviews from *School Library Journal*

features another cousin who can fade but who is certainly mad and possibly possessed. So the novel has a bit of many things: magic, murder, mystery, history, romance, diabolical possession, sex (not a lot, but what there is is explicit), and even a touch of incest. The character of Paul is developed especially well. The story is too long, and the plot is too contrived to be taken seriously, but *Fade* is riveting enough to be appreciated by Cormier fans. —Robert E. Unsworth, Scarsdale Junior High School, New York.

Selected reviews from *School Library Journal* reproduced with permission from *School Library Journal* copyright © 1977, 1988, 1997, 1999, 2001 by Cahners Business Information, a division of Reed Elsevier Inc.

List of Selected Works

After the First Death. New York: Pantheon Books, 1979.
Beyond the Chocolate War: A Novel. New York: Knopf, 1985.
The Bumblebee Flies Anyway. New York: Pantheon Books, 1983.
The Chocolate War. New York: Knopf, 1974.
Eight Plus One. New York: Pantheon Books, 1980.
Fade. New York: Delacorte Press, 1988.
Frenchtown Summer. New York: Delacorte Press, 1999.
Heroes. New York: Delacorte Press, 1998.
I Am the Cheese. New York: Knopf, 1977.
In the Middle of the Night. New York: Delacorte Press, 1995.

List of Selected Works

A Little Raw on Monday Mornings. New York: Sheed and Ward, 1963.

Now and at the Hour. New York: Coward-McCann, 1960.

Other Bells for Us to Ring. New York: Delacorte Press, 1990.

The Rag and Bone Shop. New York: Delacorte Press, 2001.

Take Me Where the Good Times Are. New York: Macmillan, 1965.

Tenderness. New York: Delacorte Press, 1997.

Tunes for Bears to Dance To. New York: Delacorte Press, 1992.

We All Fall Down. New York: Delacorte Press, 1991.

List of Selected Awards

ALAN (Assembly on Literature for Adolescents) Award in honor of outstanding contributions to the field of adolescent literature (1982)

Margaret A. Edwards Award, in honor of an author's lifetime achievement for writing books that have been popular with teenagers (1981)

After the First Death (1979)
American Library Association 100 Best Books for Teens (1966–2000)
American Library Association Best Book for Young Adults (1979)
New York Times Outstanding Book of the Year (1979)

Beyond the Chocolate War (1985)
Horn Book Honor List Citation (1986)

The Chocolate War (1974)
American Library Association 100 Best Books for Teens (1966–2000)
American Library Association Best Book for

Young Adults (1974)
Lewis Carroll Shelf Award (1979)
New York Times Outstanding Book of the Year (1974)

Eight Plus One **(1980)**
Notable Children's Trade Book in the Field of Social Studies (1980)

Fade **(1988)**
American Library Association 100 Best Books for Teens (1966–2000)
American Library Association Best Book for Young Adults (1988)

Frenchtown Summer **(1999)**
Los Angeles Times Book Prize for Young Adult Fiction (2000)

I Am the Cheese **(1977)**
American Library Association 100 Best Books for Teens (1966–2000)
American Library Association Best Book for Young Adults (1977)
New York Times Outstanding Book of the Year (1977)

The Rag and Bone Shop **(2001)**
American Library Association Top Ten Young Adult Books (2002)
American Library Association Best Books for Young Adults (2002)

Tenderness **(1997)**
American Library Association Top Ten Books for Young Adults (1998)
American Library Association Best Books for Young Adults (1998)

Glossary

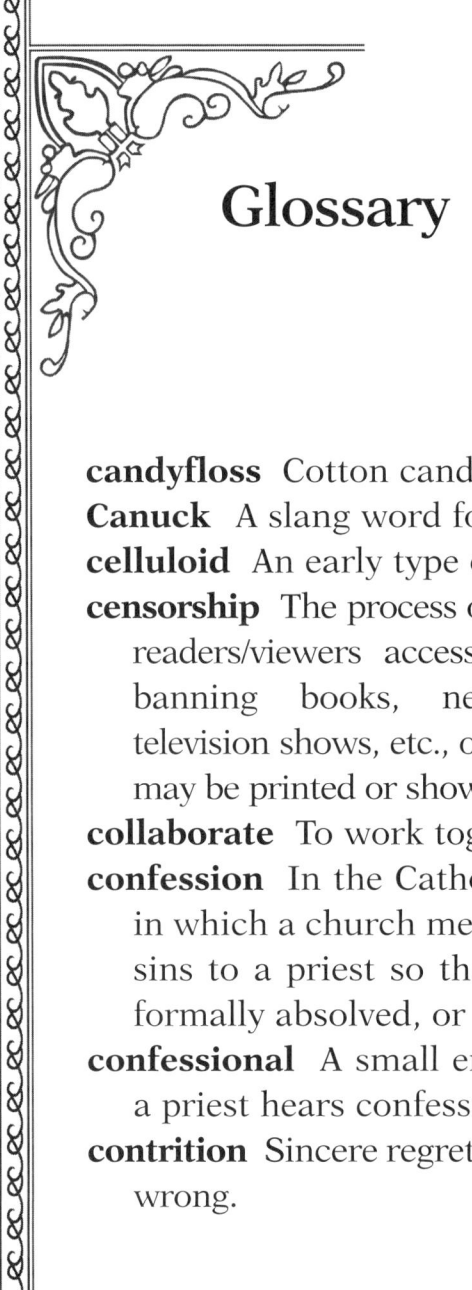

candyfloss Cotton candy.
Canuck A slang word for a Canadian.
celluloid An early type of plastic.
censorship The process of limiting or denying readers/viewers access to information by banning books, newspapers, movies, television shows, etc., or by controlling what may be printed or shown.
collaborate To work together.
confession In the Catholic Church, a ritual in which a church member tells his or her sins to a priest so that he or she can be formally absolved, or forgiven.
confessional A small enclosed place where a priest hears confessions.
contrition Sincere regret for doing something wrong.

Glossary

ecstatic Extremely happy.

Eliot, T. S. An American-born poet who became a British subject. He lived from 1888 to 1965 and is best known for his works "The Love Song of J. Alfred Prufrock" (which is the source for the quotation on Jerry's poster) and *The Wasteland*.

Great Depression A time of hardship in the United States during the 1930s when unemployment was very high and many businesses failed.

hectic Wildly energetic.

inherent Naturally a part of something.

insomnia The inability to sleep.

interim Interval, the time between one thing and another.

mandatory Required or necessary.

metaphor A direct comparison claiming that one thing is another. ("Juliet is the sun" is a metaphor.)

paradox A statement or an observation that seems contradictory or false but that may in fact be true.

paramount Of primary concern or importance.

parochial Related to religion.

poignant Touching.

protagonist Main character.

pseudonym A false name under which an author publishes his or her work.

purgatory In Catholic teaching, a temporary state or place after death where the soul can be cleansed of its sins by suffering.

Saroyan, William An Armenian American writer who lived from 1908 to 1981, known for his short stories and plays about ordinary people.

simile A comparison of two different things using the terms "like" or "as." ("My love is like a red, red rose" is a simile.)

subplot A series of events in a book that tells a story not central to the main action.

tenement A building rented to two or more families. "Tenement" is often, but not always, used to describe a crowded, rundown apartment building.

transcript A written record of a spoken conversation.

tyranny Using unjust power over another person.

Wolfe, Thomas An American author who lived from 1900 to 1938, famous for his novels based on his own life, especially his first, *Look Homeward, Angel*.

For More Information

Web Sites

Due to the changing nature of Internet links, the Rosen Publishing Group, Inc., has developed an online list of Web sites related to the subject of this book. This site is updated regularly. Please use this link to access the list:

http://www.rosenlinks.com/lab/rcor/

For Further Reading

Campbell, Patricia J. *Presenting Robert Cormier* (Twayne's United States Authors Series, Young Adult Authors). Boston: Twayne Publishers, 1989.

Hile, Kevin S., ed. *Something About the Author.* Vol. 83. New York: Gale Research, 1996, pp. 35–41.

Silvey, Anita. "An Interview with Robert Cormier." *Horn Book Magazine.* Part 1: March/April 1985, pp. 145–155. Part 2: May/June 1985, pp. 289–296.

Sutton, Roger. "King of a Funny Dichotomy: A Conversation with Robert Cormier." *School Library Journal*, June 1991, pp. 28–33.

West, Mark. *Trust Your Children: Voices Against Censorship in Children's Literature.* New York: Neal-Schuman Publishers, Inc., 1997.

Bibliography

Bagnall, Norma. "Realism: How Realistic Is It? A Look at *The Chocolate War.*" *Top of the News*, Winter 1980, p. 214.

Burns, Mary M. "Review of *Beyond the Chocolate War.*" *Horn Book Magazine*, July/August 1985, p. 451.

Campbell, Patricia J. *Presenting Robert Cormier* (Twayne's United States Authors Series, Young Adult Authors). Boston: Twayne Publishers, 1989.

Campbell Patty. "Review of *Frenchtown Summer.*" *Horn Book Magazine*, September/October 1999, p. 608.

Cart, Michael. *From Romance to Realism: 50 Years of Growth and Change in Young Adult Literature.* New York: HarperCollins Publishers, 1996.

Carter, Betty, and Karen Harris. "Realism in Adolescent Fiction: In Defense of *The Chocolate War*." *Top of the News*, Spring 1980, p. 283.

Cormier, Robert. *Beyond the Chocolate War: A Novel*. New York: Laurel-Leaf Books, 1986.

Cormier, Robert. *The Bumblebee Flies Anyway*. New York: Laurel-Leaf Books, 1993.

Cormier, Robert. *The Chocolate War*. New York: Knopf, 1974.

Cormier, Robert. "Creating *Fade*." *Horn Book Magazine*, March/April 1989, p. 166.

Cormier, Robert. *Eight Plus One*. New York, Laurel-Leaf Books, 1991.

Cormier, Robert. *Fade*. New York: Delacorte Press, 1988.

Cormier, Robert. "Forever Pedaling on the Road to Realism." *In Celebrating Children's Books: Essays on Children's Literature in Honor of Zena Sutherland*. Betsy Hearne and Marilyn Kaye, eds. New York: Lothrop, Lee, & Shepard Books, 1981, p. 45.

Cormier, Robert. *Heroes*. New York: Delacorte Press, 1998.

Cormier, Robert. *I Am the Cheese*. New York: Knopf, 1977.

Cormier, Robert, and Constance Senay Cormier, ed. *I Have Words to Spend:*

Bibliography

Reflections of a Small-Town Editor. New York: Delacorte Press, 1991.

Cormier, Robert. "Meet the Bully." *Fitchburg Sentinel and Express*, April 11, 1974. Reprinted in *I Have Words to Spend: Reflections of a Small-Town Editor* by Robert Cormier, Constance Senay Cormier, ed. New York: Delacorte Press, 1991.

Cormier, Robert. "Saying Thank You." *Fitchburg Sentinel and Express*, January 6, 1978. Reprinted in *I Have Words to Spend: Reflections of a Small-Town Editor* by Robert Cormier, Constance Senay Cormier, ed. New York: Delacorte Press, 1991.

DeLuca, Geraldine, and Roni Natov. "An Interview with Robert Cormier." *The Lion and the Unicorn*, Fall 1978, p. 109.

Foerstel, Herbert N. *Banned in the U.S.A.: A Reference Guide to Book Censorship in School and Public Libraries.* Westport, CT: Greenwood Press, 1994.

Glick, Andrea. "Robert Cormier Dead at 75." *School Library Journal*, December 2000, p. 24.

Hearne, Betsy. "Whammo, You Lose." *Booklist*, July 1, 1974, p. 1,199.

Heins, Paul. "Review of *I Am the Cheese.*" *Horn Book Magazine*. August 1977, p. 427.

Laski, Audrey. "No Laughing Matter." *Times Educational Supplement*, November 18, 1977, p. 34.

Peck, Richard. "Delivering the Goods." *American Libraries*, October 1974, p. 492.

Polacheck, Janet. Letter. *Top of the News*, Summer 1980, p. 343.

Salway, Lance. "Death and Destruction." *Times Literary Supplement*, December 2, 1977, p. 1415.

Schwartz, Tony. "Teen-agers' Laureate." *Newsweek*, July 16, 1979, p. 87.

Silvey, Anita. "An Interview with Robert Cormier: Part 1." *Horn Book Magazine*, March/April 1985, p. 145.

Silvey, Anita. "An Interview with Robert Cormier: Part 2." *Horn Book Magazine*, May/June 1985, p. 289.

Sutton, Roger. "Kind of a Funny Dichotomy: A Conversation with Robert Cormier." *School Library Journal*, June 1991, p. 28.

Veglahn, Nancy. "The Bland Face of Evil in the Novels of Robert Cormier." *Lion and the Unicorn*, June 1988, p. 12.

West, Mark. *Trust Your Children: Voices Against Censorship in Children's Literature.* New York: Neal-Schuman Publishers, Inc., 1997.

Source Notes

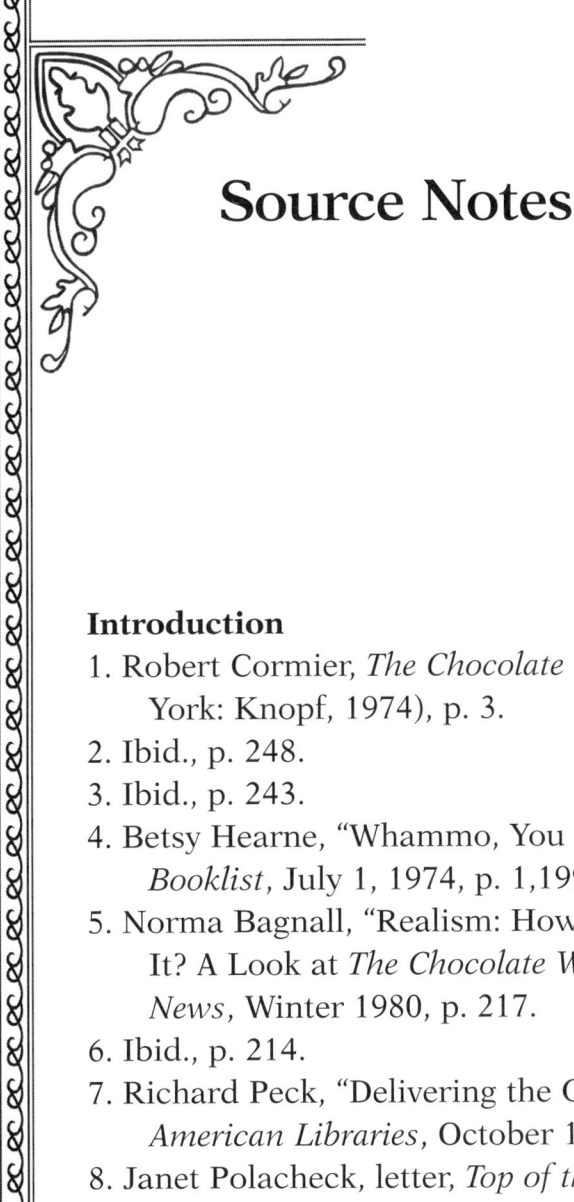

Introduction
1. Robert Cormier, *The Chocolate War* (New York: Knopf, 1974), p. 3.
2. Ibid., p. 248.
3. Ibid., p. 243.
4. Betsy Hearne, "Whammo, You Lose," *Booklist*, July 1, 1974, p. 1,199.
5. Norma Bagnall, "Realism: How Realistic Is It? A Look at *The Chocolate War*," *Top of the News*, Winter 1980, p. 217.
6. Ibid., p. 214.
7. Richard Peck, "Delivering the Goods," *American Libraries*, October 1974, p. 492.
8. Janet Polacheck, letter, *Top of the News*, Summer 1980, p. 343.
9. Anita Silvey, "An Interview with Robert

Cormier: Part 1," *Horn Book Magazine*, March/April 1985, p. 155.
10. Geraldine DeLuca and Roni Natov, "An Interview with Robert Cormier," *Lion and the Unicorn*, Fall 1978, p. 114.
11. Mark West, *Trust Your Children: Voices Against Censorship in Children's Literature* (New York: Neal-Schuman Publishers, Inc., 1997), p. 68.
12. Ibid, p. 73.

Chapter 1

1. Roger Sutton, "Kind of a Funny Dichotomy: A Conversation with Robert Cormier," *School Library Journal*, June 1991, p. 31.
2. Robert Cormier, *Fade* (New York: Delacorte Press, 1988), p. 64.
3. Robert Cormier, "The Ghost at Dusk," *St. Anthony Messenger*, January 1972, reprinted in *I Have Words to Spend: Reflections of a Small-Town Editor* by Robert Cormier, Constance Senay Cormier, ed. (New York: Delacorte Press, 1991), p. 7.
4. Robert Cormier, "Going Home Again," *Fitchburg Sentinel and Express*, July 18, 1972, reprinted in *I Have Words to Spend: Reflections of a Small-Town Editor* by Robert Cormier, Constance Senay Cormier, ed. (New York: Delacorte Press, 1991), pp. 29–30.
5. Robert Cormier, "Christmas—Now and Then," *Fitchburg Sentinel and Express*, December 21,

Source Notes

1972, reprinted in *I Have Words to Spend: Reflections of a Small-Town Editor* by Robert Cormier, Constance Senay Cormier, ed. (New York: Delacorte Press, 1991), p. 19.

6. Robert Cormier, "Sweet Sadness," *St. Anthony Messenger*, September 1976, reprinted in *I Have Words to Spend: Reflections of a Small-Town Editor* by Robert Cormier, Constance Senay Cormier, ed. (New York: Delacorte Press, 1991), p. 24.
7. Sutton, p. 32.
8. Robert Cormier, "Creating *Fade*." *Horn Book Magazine*, March/April 1989, p. 169.
9. Patricia J. Campbell, *Presenting Robert Cormier*, Twayne's United States Authors Series, Young Adult Authors, (Boston: Twayne Publishers, 1989), p. 38.
10. Sutton, p. 29.
11. Campbell, p. 17.
12. Robert Cormier, "Saying Thank You," *Fitchburg Sentinel and Express*, January 6, 1978, reprinted in *I Have Words to Spend: Reflections of a Small-Town Editor* by Robert Cormier, Constance Senay Cormier, ed. (New York: Delacorte Press, 1991), p. 93.
13. Robert Cormier, "The Cowboy Hat," *St. Anthony Messenger*, April 1975, reprinted in *I Have Words to Spend: Reflections of a Small-Town Editor* by Robert Cormier, Constance

Senay Cormier, ed.(New York: Delacorte Press, 1991), p. 27.
14. Cormier, "The Ghost at Dusk," pp. 8–9.
15. Cormier, "Saying Thank You," p. 93.

Chapter 2

1. Roger Sutton, "Kind of a Funny Dichotomy: A Conversation with Robert Cormier," *School Library Journal*, June 1991, p. 28.
2. Robert Cormier, "Meet the Bully," *Fitchburg Sentinel and Express*, April 11, 1974, reprinted in *I Have Words to Spend: Reflections of a Small-Town Editor* by Robert Cormier, Constance Senay Cormier, ed. (New York: Delacorte Press, 1991), p. 12.
3. Robert Cormier, "Creating *Fade*," *Horn Book Magazine*, March/April 1989, p. 169.
4. Robert Cormier, *Fade* (New York: Delacorte Press, 1988), pp. 105–106.
5. Robert Cormier, "The Ghost at Dusk," *St. Anthony Messenger*, January 1972, reprinted in *I Have Words to Spend: Reflections of a Small-Town Editor* by Robert Cormier, Constance Senay Cormier, ed. (New York: Delacorte Press, 1991), pp. 7–8.
6. Cormier, "Creating *Fade*," p. 170.

Chapter 3

1. Robert Cormier, "The Sound of Glass Breaking," *Fitchburg Sentinel and Express*, May 23, 1973,

Source Notes

reprinted in *I Have Words to Spend: Reflections of a Small-Town Editor* by Robert Cormier, Constance Semay Cormier, ed. (New York: Delacorte Press, 1991), pp. 41–42.

2. Roger Sutton, "Kind of a Funny Dichotomy: A Conversation with Robert Cormier," *School Library Journal*, June 1991, pp. 32–33.
3. Robert Cormier, *The Bumblebee Flies Anyway* (New York: Laurel-Leaf Books, 1993).
4. Robert Cormier, Constance Senay Cormier, ed. *I Have Words to Spend: Reflections of a Small-Town Editor* (New York: Delacorte Press, 1991), p. xiii.
5. Robert Cormier, "Keep the Faith, Baby," *Fitchburg Sentinel and Express*, September 2, 1971, reprinted in *I Have Words to Spend: Reflections of a Small-Town Editor* by Robert Cormier, Constance Senay Cormier, ed. (New York: Delacorte Press, 1991), pp. 200–202.
6. Patricia J. Campbell, *Presenting Robert Cormier*, Twayne's United States Authors Series, Young Adult Authors (Boston: Twayne Publishers, 1989), p. 21.
7. Ibid., p. 34.
8. Robert Cormier, "Christmas—Now and Then," *The Fitchburg Sentinel and Express*, December 21, 1972, reprinted in *I Have Words to Spend: Reflections of a Small-Town Editor* by Robert Cormier, Constance Senay Cormier, ed. (New York: Delacorte Press, 1991), p. 17.

9. Robert Cormier, "Those Who Don't Make Headlines," *Fitchburg Sentinel and Express*, October 31, 1972, reprinted in *I Have Words to Spend: Reflections of a Small-Town Editor* by Robert Cormier, Constance Senay Cormier, ed. (New York: Delacorte Press, 1991), p. 37.
10. Robert Cormier, *Eight Plus One* (New York, Laurel-Leaf Books, 1991), p. 5.

Chapter 4

1. Mark West, *Trust Your Children: Voices Against Censorship in Children's Literature* (New York: Neal-Schuman Publishers, Inc., 1997), p. 68.
2. Robert Cormier, "Father of the Groom," *Fitchburg Sentinel and Express*, January 6, 1978, reprinted in *I Have Words to Spend: Reflections of a Small-Town Editor* by Robert Cormier, Constance Senay Cormier, ed. (New York: Delacorte Press, 1991), p. 91.
3. Geraldine DeLuca and Roni Natov, "An Interview with Robert Cormier," *Lion and the Unicorn*, Fall 1978, p. 109.
4. Michael Cart, *From Romance to Realism: 50 Years of Growth and Change in Young Adult Literature* (New York: HarperCollins Publishers, 1996), pp. 43–44.
5. Anita Silvey, "An Interview with Robert Cormier: Part 2," *Horn Book Magazine*, May/June 1985, p. 293.

Source Notes

6. Robert Cormier, introduction to *I Am the Cheese* (New York: Knopf, 1977).
7. Cormier, *I Am the Cheese*, pp. 3–4.
8. DeLuca and Natov, pp. 123–124.
9. Audrey Laski, "No Laughing Matter," *Times Educational Supplement*, November 18, 1977, p. 34.
10. Lance Salway, "Death and Destruction," *Times Literary Supplement*, December 2, 1977, p. 1,415.
11. Paul Heins, "Review of *I Am the Cheese*," *Horn Book Magazine*, August 1977, pp. 427–428.
12. West, p. 76.
13. Patricia J. Campbell, *Presenting Robert Cormier*, Twayne's United States Authors Series, Young Adult Authors (Boston: Twayne Publishers, 1989), p. 11.
14. Ibid, p. 161.

Chapter 5

1. Anita Silvey, "An Interview with Robert Cormier: Part 2," *Horn Book Magazine*, May/June 1985, p. 295.
2. Robert Cormier, introduction to *I Am the Cheese* (New York: Knopf, 1977).
3. Silvey, "An Interview with Robert Cormier: Part 2," p. 296.
4. Ibid., p. 291.
5. Robert Cormier, "Creating *Fade*," *Horn Book Magazine*, March/April 1989, p. 172.

6. Ibid., p. 172.
7. Silvey, "An Interview with Robert Cormier: Part 2," p. 289.
8. Ibid., p. 290.
9. Robert Cormier, *Eight Plus One* (New York, Laurel-Leaf Books, 1991), p. 70.
10. Silvey, "An Interview with Robert Cormier: Part 2," p. 289.
11. Cormier, "Creating *Fade*," p. 171.
12. Silvey, "An Interview with Robert Cormier, Part 2," p. 296.
13. Ibid., p. 296.
14. Tony Schwartz, "Teen-agers' Laureate," *Newsweek*, July 16, 1979, p. 87.
15. Anita Silvey, "An Interview with Robert Cormier: Part 1," *Horn Book Magazine*, March/April 1985, p. 145.
16. Ibid., p. 151.
17. Ibid., p. 147.
18. Mary M. Burns, "Review of *Beyond the Chocolate War*," *Horn Book Magazine*, July/August 1985, p. 453.
19. Patty Campbell, "Review of *Frenchtown Summer*," *Horn Book Magazine*, September/October 1999, p. 608.
20. Andrea Glick, "Robert Cormier Dead at 75," *School Library Journal*, December 2000, p. 24.

Source Notes

Chapter 6

1. Nancy Veglahn, "The Bland Face of Evil in the Novels of Robert Cormier," *Lion and the Unicorn*, June 1988, p. 12.
2. Roger Sutton, "Kind of a Funny Dichotomy: A Conversation with Robert Cormier," *School Library Journal*, June 1991, p. 29.
3. Anita Silvey, "An Interview with Robert Cormier: Part 1," *Horn Book Magazine*, March/April 1985, p. 154.
4. Sutton, pp. 29–30.
5. Silvey, "An Interview with Robert Cormier: Part 1," p. 147.
6. Ibid., p. 155.
7. Robert Cormier, "Meet the Bully," *Fitchburg Sentinel and Express*, April 11, 1974, reprinted in *I Have Words to Spend: Reflections of a Small-Town Editor* by Robert Cormier, Constance Senay Cormier, ed. (New York: Delacorte Press, 1991), p. 13.
8. Robert Cormier, "In the Nation's Capitol," *Fitchburg Sentinel and Express*, April 8, 1977, reprinted in *I Have Words to Spend: Reflections of a Small-Town Editor* by Robert Cormier, Constance Senay Cormier, ed. (New York: Delacorte Press, 1991), p. 108.
9. Silvey, p. 152.

10. Robert Cormier, *Beyond the Chocolate War* (New York: Laurel-Leaf Books, 1986), pp. 263–264.
11. Silvey, p. 155.
12. Betty Carter and Karen Harris, "Realism in Adolescent Fiction: In Defense of *The Chocolate War*," *Top of the News*, Spring 1980, p. 285.

Chapter 7

1. American Library Association, "Robert Cormier Named Edwards Award Winner," Retrieved February 21, 2002 (http://www.ala.org/yalsa/edwards/cormier.html).
2. Norma Bagnall, "Realism: How Realistic Is It? A Look at *The Chocolate War*," *Top of the News*, Winter 1980, p. 214.
3. Anita Silvey, "An Interview with Robert Cormier: Part 2," *Horn Book Magazine*, May/June 1985, p. 292.
4. Robert Cormier, *The Chocolate War* (New York: Knopf, 1974), p. 3.
5. Robert Cormier, *Beyond The Chocolate War: A Novel* (New York: Laurel-Leaf Books, 1986), p. 3.
6. Robert Cormier, *Heroes* (New York: Delacorte Press, 1998), p. 1.
7. Geraldine DeLuca and Roni Natov, "An Interview with Robert Cormier," *Lion and the Unicorn*, Fall 1978, pp. 133–134.
8. Ibid., p. 112.

Source Notes

9. Robert Cormier, "Forever Pedaling on the Road to Realism," in *Celebrating Children's Books: Essays On Children's Literature in Honor of Zena Sutherland*. Betsy Hearne and Marilyn Kaye, eds. (New York: Lothrop, Lee, & Shepard Books, 1981), pp. 48–49.
10. Roger Sutton, "Kind of a Funny Dichotomy: A Conversation with Robert Cormier," *School Library Journal*, June 1991, p. 30.
11. Andrea Glick, "Robert Cormier Dead at 75," *School Library Journal*, December 2000, p. 24.

Index

A
Act of Contrition, 35
Adventures of Tom Sawyer, The, 20, 42
After the First Death, 34, 54–55, 62, 66, 69
American Library Association, 10, 11, 13
"And So On" (column), 33
Associated Press Award of New England, 32–33

B
Bagnall, Norma, 11–12, 64, 67
Beyond the Chocolate War, 52, 55–56, 60, 62–63, 67
Bumblebee Flies Anyway, The, 32, 55

C
Chocolate War, The, 7–10, 39, 47, 51, 56, 58, 59–60, 62, 64, 66, 67, 69
  censorship of, 13
  movie adaptation of, 49
  reviews/critical response to, 9, 10–12, 44
  sequel to, 44, 55–56
  writing and publication of, 40, 41–42, 43–44
Coen, Fabio, 43, 46, 47
Cormier, Connie (wife), 30–31, 32, 33, 59
Cormier, Robert
  adult novels by, 35, 37–38, 49, 57
  and Catholicism, 19, 31–32
  childhood of, 15–22, 23–28
  journalism awards won by, 32–33
  marriage and children of, 30–31, 32, 33, 37–38, 40, 41, 54
  short stories of, 29, 34–35, 41, 49, 55

Index

villains of, 58–61, 62
writing routine of, 50–51
YA novels of, 7, 13–14, 16, 32, 33–34, 43–44, 46–47, 49, 54, 55, 56–57

E
Eight Plus One, 37–38, 55

F
Fade, 16, 26–27, 70
Family Friendly Libraries, 13
Fitchburg Sentinel, 32–33
Frenchtown Summer, 56

H
Heroes, 67–68
Hinton, S. E., 42, 66

I
I Am the Cheese, 50, 51, 60, 62, 66, 69
  censorship of, 13
  movie adaptation of, 49
  reviews/critical response to, 47
  writing and publication of, 45–47

L
Leominster Daily Enterprise, 27
Little Raw on Monday Mornings, A, 37
"Little Things That Count, The," 29, 34
Little Women, 42

M
Margaret A. Edwards Award, 66
Marlow, Marilyn, 36, 37, 43

N
Now and at the Hour, 37

O
Outsiders, The, 42

P
Peck, Richard, 11, 66
problem novel, explanation of, 42–43

R
Rag and Bone Shop, The, 57

S
Saroyan, William, 21
Seventeenth Summer, 42
Sign, The, 29, 34

T
Take Me Where the Good Times Are, 37
Tenderness, 33, 57

W
We All Fall Down, 57
Wolfe, Thomas, 21
Worcester Telegram and Gazette, 31, 32

Y
YA novel, explanation of, 41–42

Z
Zindel, Paul, 66

About the Author

Sarah L. Thomson is the author of *The Dragon's Son*, a retelling of the King Arthur legend for young adult readers, which received a starred review from the *Bulletin of the Center for Children's Books*. She has also written *The Library of Author Biographies: Gary Paulsen* and *Stars and Stripes: The Story of the American Flag*. After graduating from Oberlin College in Oberlin, Ohio, she moved to New York City to become an editor of children's books. She now works full-time as a writer and lives in Brooklyn with her two cats, who help with her writing by lying on the piece of paper she needs most.

Editor

Annie Sommers

Photo Credits

Cover © James Patrick Langlands; p. 2 © AP/Wide World Photos.

Series Design and Layout

Tahara Hasan

PROPERTY OF ST. JOHN'S
LUTHERAN SCHOOL LIBRARY
3* * JEFFCO BLVD.
* *LD, MO 63010